Anxiety Disorders Interview Schedule for DSM-IV

Child Version

Child Interview Schedule

Wendy K. Silverman
Anne Marie Albano

OXFORD
UNIVERSITY PRESS

OXFORD
UNIVERSITY PRESS

Oxford University Press, Inc., publishes works that further
Oxford University's objective of excellence
in research, scholarship, and education.

Oxford   New York
Auckland   Cape Town   Dar es Salaam   Hong Kong   Karachi
Kuala Lumpur   Madrid   Melbourne   Mexico City   Nairobi
New Delhi   Shanghai   Taipei   Toronto

With offices in
Argentina   Austria   Brazil   Chile   Czech Republic   France   Greece
Guatemala   Hungary   Italy   Japan   Poland   Portugal   Singapore
South Korea   Switzerland   Thailand   Turkey   Ukraine   Vietnam

Published by Oxford University Press, Inc.
198 Madison Avenue, New York, New York 10016

www.oup.com

Oxford is a registered trademark of Oxford University Press

ISBN-13 978-0-19-518383-2
ISBN 0-19-518383-5

9 8 7 6 5 4 3 2

Printed in the United States of America
on acid-free paper

Contents

Series Introduction

The diagnostic assessment program in this Child Interview Schedule is part of a series of empirically supported treatment and assessment programs. The purpose of the series is to disseminate knowledge about specific assessments and interventions for which systematic research studies indicate effectiveness. This assessment program, along with others in the series, has been demonstrated to have empirical support for its efficacy in assessing the particular condition you are addressing. However, clinicians operate with a wide variety of patients with different characteristics who are treated in different types of settings. Thus, the manner in which the assessment program is implemented will be the decision of the clinician with his or her unparalleled knowledge of the local clinical situation and the particular patient under care. Although some data indicate that allegiance to the assessment protocol produces the best results in a variety of clinical settings, only the clinician is in a position to judge the degree of flexibility required to achieve optimal results.

We sincerely hope that you find the program, of which this Child Interview Schedule forms an integral part, useful in your clinical practice. This assessment program is one of several assessment programs for the diagnosis of anxiety disorders and screening of other related disorders. These assessments have been carefully coordinated with the *DSM–IV* for consistently accurate diagnoses for treatment planning and research.

For information on the theoretical approach and empirical work that supports this assessment program, please refer to the Clinician Manual. We encourage review of the Clinician Manual and its references for a comprehensive understanding. Please let us know if you have suggestions for improving our systems for helping you deliver effective psychosocial assessments and treatments for patients under your care.

David H. Barlow, PhD
Distinguished Professor

About the Authors

WENDY K. SILVERMAN, PhD, is professor of psychology and Director of the Child and Family Psychosocial Research Center at Florida International University of Miami. Dr. Silverman has received several grants from the National Institute of Mental Health to design and evaluate psychosocial interventions for children with anxiety disorders. She has published numerous articles and chapters as well as the books *Anxiety and Phobic Disorders: A Pragmatic Approach,* with William M. Kurtines, and *Developmental Issues in the Clinical Treatment of Children and Adolescents,* coedited with Thomas H. Ollendick.

ANNE MARIE ALBANO, PhD, is currently an assistant professor of psychology and Co-Director of the Anxiety Research and Treatment Center at the University of Louisville. Dr. Albano is the former program director of the Child and Adolescent Anxiety Disorders Program of the Center for Stress and Anxiety Disorders in Albany, New York. She has published widely in the area of childhood anxiety disorders.

For specific instructions and guidelines concerning the administration of this instrument, consult the Clinician Manual for *Anxiety Disorders Interview Schedule for DSM–IV: Child Version.*

Child's Name: _____ Date of Interview: _____

Gender: _____ Date of Birth: _____ Age: _____

Race/Ethnicity: _____ Religious Affiliation: _____

Case Number: _____
(to facilitate tracking with matching Parent Interview Schedule)

Interviewer: _____

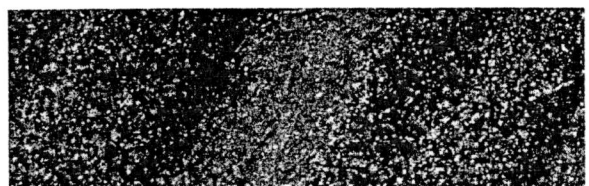

Introduction

The interviewer should begin with a brief introduction and explanation of the purpose of the interview. Obtain a brief description of the presenting complaint, leaving details to be covered by the interview in later questions.

I would like to get a general idea about the sort of things that have been bothering you and why you think you are here today.

_____

_____

_____

_____

_____

Okay, I have some other questions that I would like to ask you, and we will get back to what you just told me later.

During the time that we'll be together, I might use different words to ask you if you are afraid. For younger children, ask, **What other words might you use to say that you're afraid?** The interviewer should elicit words such as _scared, nervous, frightened,_ and so on, and clarify their meaning, as necessary. **So, feeling afraid, nervous, scared, and frightened are the types of feelings that we will be talking about today, okay?**

Now, as I said, I have a lot of questions here. Sometimes you might have a lot to tell me, and other times you might have very little to say. That's because some of the questions might really be about things that make you nervous or scared, but some are not. Also, I think what you say is important, so I will be writing things down so I don't forget, okay?

Also, (child's name), before we begin, it is very important for you to realize that there are no right or wrong answers to these questions.

Throughout the interview, some questions will represent symptoms or criteria for diagnostic categories and are followed by

"Yes," "No," and "Other" responses. For some criteria, a certain number of symptoms must be endorsed before those criteria can be assigned. To facilitate the counting of those symptoms, a circle for each symptom is provided in the right margin to be checked when a child endorses the symptom. If the question or series of questions represents a criterion, the question or series of questions is followed by a diamond that the interviewer checks when the child endorses it. If all required criteria (diamonds) are endorsed, the interviewer may place a check mark in the star at the end of each section to indicate a possible diagnosis of that category.

The following instructions should be supplemented by the interviewer's use of the visual prompt, the Feelings Thermometer (found on the back cover of the Clinician Manual). The interviewer should point to appropriate levels on the thermometer.

At different times, I will be asking you to tell me how nervous or afraid you are. To help you show me how you feel, we will use this picture of thermometers. Do you know what a thermometer does? Well, this Feelings Thermometer works somewhat like a real thermometer does. If I had a real thermometer, I could put it in your mouth and it would measure your temperature, from very low to very high. Well, with this Feelings Thermometer, we measure how afraid or nervous you are, from *not at all* to *very, very much,* by your pointing to the number on the thermometer that best shows how you feel.

At this point the interviewer should explain the 9-point scale, from 0 *(Not at all)* to 8 *(Very, very much),* and should demonstrate the Feelings Thermometer, explaining how the more "mercury" that appears means more feeling, that is, that "you are more scared," just like a regular thermometer. The interviewer then gives practice examples and ensures the child's understanding of the scale.

Okay, (child's name), **now that you understand how the thermometer measures feelings, let's practice with a few examples.** (See Clinician Manual for more examples.) Allow the child to respond after each question.

How afraid or nervous are you when you are eating your favorite dessert?

How afraid or nervous are you when you are riding on a roller coaster?

I will also ask you to tell me how much your feelings mess things up for you. So, if you are scared or worried about something, I want to know how much those feelings keep you from having fun, doing your school work or assignments, or cause you to be upset or feel bad. We'll use the thermometer for this, too. For example, if I ask a person who is afraid of dogs how much that messes things up for him or her, then he or she might tell me "A lot" (point to *A lot* on the thermometer) if it keeps him or her from playing with friends, walking to school, or going on outings. For example, if a friend of yours has a dog that barks a lot and you are very afraid of it, you might stay away from or avoid going to your friend's house. But if it only bothers you a little and you are able to go to your friend's house anyway, you might say "Not at all" or "A little bit." Do you understand?

I am also going to ask you to tell me how long something has been bothering you. Sometimes I will want to know if it has been bothering you for a whole week, or maybe two weeks, or even for a month. So now, let's figure out together what kind of things have happened over the past few months (use Side 1 of the ADIS for DSM–IV:C Calendar at the back of this interview schedule). Obtain temporal prompts for potentially critical events such as a birthdays, major holidays, school vacations, and anniversaries of major losses and transitions to use later in the interview in the assessment of duration of a particular disorder (record these events on Side 2 of the ADIS for DSM–IV:C Calendar). Okay, later on I will be asking you whether something has been going on or bothering you since (mention a critical date). Do you have any questions about that?

Background Information

1. **Do you have a nickname or should I just call you** (child's name)?

   _____

2. **Where do you live?**

   _____

3. **What is your phone number?** _____

School History

This section contains some general questions about the child's school attendance and performance. If the child stated at the start of the interview that his or her problem is difficulty attending school, the interviewer should begin with Question 2 and restructure the format of the questions, for example, "If you were in school, which school would you go to?"

1. During school year (September–June), ask, **Do you go to school?**   ☐ Yes ☐ No ☐ Other

   During summer, ask, **Do you go to school during the school year?**

   If "No" or "Other," have the child explain:

   _____

   _____

2. **Where do you go to school?** _____

3. **What grade are you in?** _____

   During summer, **What grade will you be going into?** _____

4a. **Do you like school?**   ☐ Yes ☐ No ☐ Other

4b. **What do you like about school? What's your favorite subject?**

   _____

   _____

   _____

4c. **What don't you like about school? What's your least favorite subject?** _____

   _____

   _____

5. **What kind of grades are you getting in school?** _____

   _____

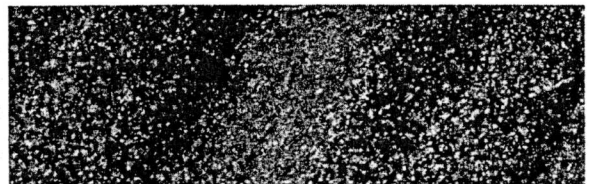

School Refusal Behavior

Initial Inquiry

1. **Do you get very nervous or scared about having to go to school?** ☐ Yes ☐ No ☐ Other

2. **Do you stay home from school because you are nervous or scared?** ☐ Yes ☐ No ☐ Other

   If "Yes," **How many times has that happened this year?** _____

   Calculate percentage of days missed in the present school year.

   _____

   How many times did that happen last year? _____

   Calculate percentage of days missed during the last school
   year. _____

3a. **Do you get very nervous or scared when you are in school?** ☐ Yes ☐ No ☐ Other

   If the child responds "Yes," ask Questions 3b and 3c. Otherwise, skip to Question 4.

3b. **When you are scared in school, do you ever go to the school nurse** ☐ Yes ☐ No ☐ Other
   or counselor?

   If "Yes," **How often?** _____

3c. **When you are scared at school, do you or does someone from** ☐ Yes ☐ No ☐ Other
   school, such as the school nurse, ever call your mom or dad?

   If "Yes," **How often has that happened this school year?**

   _____

   Ask the child to elaborate on any "Yes" response to Question
   3a, 3b, or 3c. Inquire about patterns of reassurance seeking.

How often each day or week does the child seek contact from parents or school personnel about anxiety or anxiety symptoms, physical complaints, and so on? What makes things better for the child? _____

_____

_____

4. **Has your mother, father, or someone else ever picked you up early from school because you were nervous or scared?**   ☐ Yes ☐ No ☐ Other

If "Yes," **How many times has that happened this school year?**

If "Yes" to any of Questions 1–4, go to Question 5.

If "No" to Questions 1–4, skip to Separation Anxiety Disorder (p. 11).

5. For younger children, ask, **Have you ever stayed home from school and had someone teach you at home?**   ☐ Yes ☐ No ☐ Other

For adolescents, ask, **Have you ever stayed home and had a tutor?**   ☐ Yes ☐ No ☐ Other

If "Yes" or "Other," have the child or adolescent explain:

_____

_____

6. **Do you miss school or leave school early because you like it better at home?**   ☐ Yes ☐ No ☐ Other

7. For younger children, ask, **If I had a magic wand, is there anything I could do to make school less scary?** _____

_____

For adolescents, ask, **What exactly is it that makes school scary for you?** _____

_____

_____

Fear (Yes or No)

8a. **Now I am going to read you a list of a few things** (see list following Question 8c). **These are things that kids usually find most scary about school. I'd like you to tell me if any of these things make you nervous or scared about going to school, okay?**

Record as "No" those responses that reflect "typical" child school-related anxiety (e.g., "a little nervous before tests," "a little nervous when I forget my homework") and record as "Yes" those responses that reflect excessive anxiety.

Fear Ratings (0–8)

8b. For each "Yes" response to the items in the list, use the Feelings Thermometer (found on the back cover of the Clinician Manual) to obtain fear severity ratings. Record the ratings (0–8) in the appropriate column.

For each of those things that you said scares you (or makes you nervous) about going to school, I'd like to find out how scared you get by using the Feelings Thermometer. Tell me how afraid you feel you are of (specific situation endorsed by the child in Question 8a, e.g., "talking in front of the class").

Interference Ratings (0–8)

8c. For those items in Question 8b endorsed with a severity rating of 4 *(Some)* or greater, a rating of interference should also be obtained with the Feelings Thermometer. Record the ratings (0–8) in the appropriate column. Otherwise, skip to Question 9.

Okay, now I want to know how much the fears you have told me about so far have messed things up for you in school, how much it upsets you or bothers you, how much it stops you from doing things in school you would like to do, and so on. So, tell me how much does being scared of (e.g., the teacher) **mess things up for you?**

	Fear		Fear Rating (0–8)	Interference Rating (0–8)
	Yes	No		
The teacher(s) or principal	☐	☐	☐	☐
The other kids	☐	☐	☐	☐
Speaking to other people	☐	☐	☐	☐
Having to talk in class or talk in front of the class	☐	☐	☐	☐
Taking tests	☐	☐	☐	☐
Getting good grades	☐	☐	☐	☐
Writing on the chalkboard	☐	☐	☐	☐
Being away from your parents because you are in school	☐	☐	☐	☐
The bell ringing	☐	☐	☐	☐
Gym class	☐	☐	☐	☐
Riding on the school bus	☐	☐	☐	☐
Eating in the cafeteria	☐	☐	☐	☐
Homework	☐	☐	☐	☐
Fire drills	☐	☐	☐	☐
Anything else?	☐	☐	☐	☐

9. **How long have you had problems going to** (or staying in) **school?**

_____

_____

Note. Evidence of significant school refusal behavior warrants clarification and further examination within each of the *DSM–IV* diagnostic categories. School refusal is not a diagnostic category by itself but might be a behavioral manifestation of a clinical disorder.

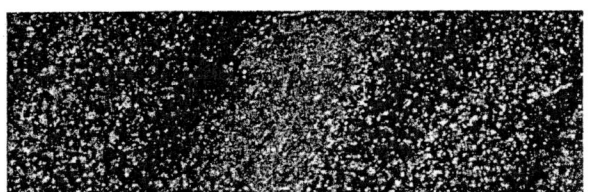

Separation Anxiety Disorder

Initial Inquiry

Some children (teenagers) **worry a lot about being away from their parents or from home.**

1a. **Do you feel really scared or worried when you are away from your mom or dad and do you do whatever you can to be with them?** ☐ Yes ☐ No ☐ Other

1b. **Do you get very upset, cry, or beg your parents to stay home when they plan to go somewhere without you?** ☐ Yes ☐ No ☐ Other

1c. **When your parents leave you, do you cry or feel very bad because you miss them a lot?** ☐ Yes ☐ No ☐ Other

1d. **When you know that you are going to be away from home or your parents, do you get very upset and worry ahead of time?** ☐ Yes ☐ No ☐ Other

Count any "Yes" response to Questions 1a–1d as one symptom and place a check mark in the circle.　　　　　　**SYMPTOM**

2a. **When you are not with your parents, do you worry a lot that something bad might happen to them, like they might get sick or hurt and die?** ☐ Yes ☐ No ☐ Other

If "Yes," **What do you think might happen to them?** _____

_____

2b. **When you are not with your parents, do you worry that they might leave and never come back?** ☐ Yes ☐ No ☐ Other

Count any "Yes" response to Questions 2a and 2b as one symptom and place a check mark in the circle.　　　　　　**SYMPTOM**

3. **Do you worry a lot that something bad might happen to you, like someone might take you or you might get lost, so you couldn't see your parents again?**   ☐ Yes ☐ No ☐ Other

   If "Yes," place a check mark in the circle.

   SYMPTOM

   If "Yes," **What do you think might happen to you?** _____
   _____
   _____

4. **Some children (teenagers) find some places hard to go to, like over to a friend's house, because they are afraid to be away from their parents. Are there any places that you won't go, because you are afraid to be away from your parents?**   ☐ Yes ☐ No ☐ Other

   If "Yes," place a check mark in the circle.

   SYMPTOM

   If "Yes," **What places won't you go to?** (Inquire about school, outings with friends, malls, etc.) _____
   _____

   If one or both circles for Questions 3 and 4 are checked, continue. Otherwise, skip to Interpersonal Relationships (p. 15).

5a. **Do you try as hard as you can to always be near your mom or dad, or someone else that you love?**   ☐ Yes ☐ No ☐ Other

5b. **Do you try as hard as you can to never be at home alone?**   ☐ Yes ☐ No ☐ Other

5c. **When you are at home with your parents, are you scared of being alone in your room or any other place in the house? For example, if your parents are on one side of the house, like in the kitchen, and you are on the other side of the house, for example, in your bedroom, do you go to the kitchen so you can be with your parents?**   ☐ Yes ☐ No ☐ Other

   Count any "Yes" response to Questions 5a–5c as one symptom and place a check mark in the circle.

   SYMPTOM

6a. **Do you often want to have your mother or dad** (or another adult) **stay close to you when it's time to go to sleep at night? For example, do you like to have someone, like your mother or father, lie down next to you when it's time to go to bed?**   ☐ Yes ☐ No ☐ Other

6b. **Is it hard for you to sleep over at other kids' houses because you are afraid to be away from your parents?**   ☐ Yes ☐ No ☐ Other

Count any "Yes" response to Questions 6a and 6b as one symptom and place a check mark in the circle.

 **SYMPTOM**

 If the child responds "Yes" to any of Questions 5 and 6, continue. Otherwise, skip to Interpersonal Relationships (p. 15).

7. **Do you have bad dreams about being away from your parent(s)?**   ☐ Yes ☐ No ☐ Other

   If "Yes," place a check mark in the circle.   **SYMPTOM**

8. **When you have to leave home to go to school or some place else, do you usually feel sick? For example, do you get stomachaches or headaches or feel like you are going to throw up?**   ☐ Yes ☐ No ☐ Other

   If "Yes," place a check mark in the circle.   **SYMPTOM**

 If three or more circles for Questions 1–8 are checked, place a check mark in the diamond and continue. Otherwise, skip to Interpersonal Relationships (p. 15).    **CRITERION**

9. **Has this feeling of being scared or worried when you are not with your parents been going on for at least four weeks?**   ☐ Yes ☐ No ☐ Other

   If "Yes," place a check mark in the diamond and continue. Otherwise skip to Interpersonal Relationships (p. 15).    **CRITERION**

To meet diagnostic criteria for Separation Anxiety Disorder, the child must respond "Yes" to at least three symptoms from Questions 1–8 and also "Yes" to Question 9. In addition, there must be evidence of significant interference in functioning, as indicated by the response in the following section.

 If symptom criteria are met (both diamonds are checked), continue. Otherwise, skip to Interpersonal Relationships (p. 15).

Interference

Okay, I want to know how much you feel this problem has messed things up in your life. That is, how much has it messed things up for you with friends, in school, or at home? How much does it stop you from doing things you would like to do? Tell me how much by using the Feelings Thermometer we discussed earlier, okay? If necessary, explain the

☐

concept of interference with the child. Show the child the Feelings Thermometer (found on the back cover of the Clinician Manual) and obtain an overall rating of interference from the child. Record the number corresponding to the child's anchor response, 0–8.

If clinical interference is indicated (a rating of 4 or greater), place a check mark in the diamond.

If all three diamonds are checked, consider Separation Anxiety Disorder diagnosis and place a check mark in the star.

Separation Anxiety Disorder

Interpersonal Relationships

Now I want to ask you some questions about friends.

1a. **First, I want to know whether you think you have more friends than most kids do, fewer than most kids do, or about the same as most kids do?**
   ☐ More than most kids
   ☐ Fewer than most kids
   ☐ The same as most kids
   ☐ Other

If the child reports "Fewer" or "No Friends," then ask Question 1b.

1b. **If you could, would you like to have more friends?**   ☐ Yes ☐ No ☐ Other

2a. **Do you have a best friend?**   ☐ Yes ☐ No ☐ Other

2b. **How long have you been friends with that person?**

3. **Do you think you have trouble making friends?**   ☐ Yes ☐ No ☐ Other

4. **Once you've made friends, do you think you have trouble keeping them?**   ☐ Yes ☐ No ☐ Other

5. **What kinds of things do you like to do with your friend(s)?** (Inquire about social activities.)

6a. **Are you in any club or group or do you play on any sports team?**   ☐ Yes ☐ No ☐ Other

6b. If "No," **Did you ever?**   ☐ Yes ☐ No ☐ Other

   If "Yes" to Question 6a or 6b, **What group(s) or sport(s) or club(s)? When?**

7. **If you had a choice, would you spend most of your time with other kids or alone?**   ☐ With other kids
   ☐ Alone ☐ Other

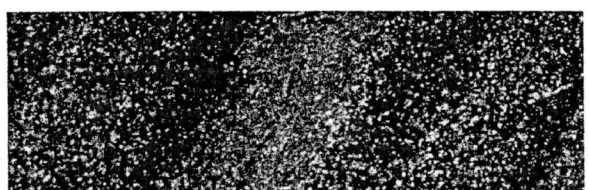

Social Phobia (Social Anxiety Disorder)

Initial Inquiry

Some kids (teenagers) **feel** *really* **scared and uncomfortable in situations with other people—so scared and uncomfortable that they might want to** *stay away* **from these places. Some kids** (teenagers) **might also cry, or even have a temper tantrum, or get angry when they have to be in situations with other people. What happens is that they might be told to go to these places, but they would rather not. They are much more afraid of these situations than other kids their age are.**

1a. **When you are in certain places with other people like school, restaurants, or parties, do you feel that people might think that something you do is stupid or dumb?**
☐ Yes ☐ No ☐ Other

If "Yes," place a check mark in the circle.
SYMPTOM

1b. **When you are in certain places with other people, like school, restaurants, or parties, do you think that people might laugh at you?**
☐ Yes ☐ No ☐ Other

If "Yes," place a check mark in the circle.
SYMPTOM

1c. **When you are in these situations with other people, do you worry that you might do something that will make you feel ashamed or embarrassed?**
☐ Yes ☐ No ☐ Other

If "Yes," place a check mark in the circle.
SYMPTOM

 If one or more "Yes" responses to Questions 1a–1c, place a check mark in the diamond.
CRITERION

For any of Questions 1a–1c that the child endorsed, the interviewer might wish to obtain further elaborations to determine if that area is clinically significant. Also, if the child responded

"No" to Questions 1a–1c, the interviewer may use discretion in inquiring about the situations listed in Question 2c.

Fear (Yes or No)

2a. **Now I am going to give you a list of some situations** (see list following Question 2c). **I want to know if you think you get more nervous or scared in these situations than other kids your age do. Answer "Yes" only if these situations almost always make you scared or nervous, not if it has just happened once or twice. First, just tell me "Yes" or "No."**

Note. The interviewer may use discretion inquiring about age-relevant situations. Those situations more common to older children and adolescents are grouped at the end of the list. Also, if the child responded "No" to Questions 1a–1c, the interviewer may use discretion in inquiring about all the situations listed.

Fear Ratings (0–8)

2b. For each situation to which the child responded "Yes," obtain fear ratings using the Feelings Thermometer (found on the back cover of the Clinician Manual). Ask, **When you say that you're afraid or nervous** (e.g., giving an oral report), **how afraid do you feel when you're** (e.g., giving an oral report)? **Use the thermometer to show me how afraid or nervous you get.**

Avoidance/Distress (Yes or No)

2c. For each situation in Question 2b with a fear rating of 4 *(Some)* or greater, inquire about avoidance behavior and endurance with distress. Ask, **For those things you rated some or more fear (4 or higher), I now want to know if you ever try to avoid or stay away from these situations** (e.g., working in groups)?

If one or more situations in the list are endorsed as either avoided or endured, place a check mark in the diamond.

CRITERION

	Fear		Fear Rating (0–8)	Avoidance/ Distress	
	Yes	No		Yes	No
Answering questions in class	☐	☐	☐	☐	☐
Giving a report or reading aloud in front of the class	☐	☐	☐	☐	☐
Asking the teacher a question or for help	☐	☐	☐	☐	☐
Taking tests	☐	☐	☐	☐	☐
Writing on the chalkboard	☐	☐	☐	☐	☐
Working or playing with a group of kids	☐	☐	☐	☐	☐
Gym class	☐	☐	☐	☐	☐
Walking in the hallways or hanging out by your locker	☐	☐	☐	☐	☐
Starting or joining in on a conversation	☐	☐	☐	☐	☐
Using school or public bathrooms	☐	☐	☐	☐	☐
Eating in front of others (e.g., home, school cafeteria, restaurants)	☐	☐	☐	☐	☐
Meetings such as girl or boy scouts or team meetings	☐	☐	☐	☐	☐
Answering or talking on the telephone	☐	☐	☐	☐	☐
Musical or athletic performances	☐	☐	☐	☐	☐
Inviting a friend to get together	☐	☐	☐	☐	☐
Speaking to adults (e.g., store clerk, waiters, principal)	☐	☐	☐	☐	☐
Talking to persons you don't know well (e.g., strangers, new or unfamiliar people)	☐	☐	☐	☐	☐
Attending parties, dances, or school activity nights	☐	☐	☐	☐	☐
Having your picture taken (e.g., for the yearbook)	☐	☐	☐	☐	☐
Dating	☐	☐	☐	☐	☐
Being asked to do something that you really don't want to do, but you can't say no. For example, if someone wants to borrow your homework or favorite toy, is it hard to say no?	☐	☐	☐	☐	☐
Having someone do something to you that you don't like, but you can't tell them to stop. For example, if someone is teasing you, is it hard for you to tell them to leave you alone?	☐	☐	☐	☐	☐

Are there any other times that being around people makes you nervous or scared?   ☐ Yes ☐ No ☐ Other

If "Yes," **Could you tell me about that?** _____

_____

_____

If the child responded "No" to any of Questions 1a–1c and reports no fear or avoidance in any situation in Questions 2a–2c, skip to Specific Phobia (p. 23).

To meet diagnostic criteria for Social Phobia, the child must respond "Yes" to at least one question from Questions 1a–1c, respond "Yes" to at least one situation listed in Question 2a, and either avoid or endure social situations with intense anxiety or distress. In addition, there must be evidence of significant interference in the child's normal routine as indicated by the response in the Interference section.

Now I want to find out more details about some of those things that bother you. When you tell me that (insert specifics of the child's fear, e.g., "you don't like to start a conversation"):

3. **Does it make a difference if the people are friends or strangers?**   ☐ Yes ☐ No ☐ Other

   If "Yes," **Which is easier?**
   ☐ Friends   ☐ Strangers

4. **Does it make a difference if the group is boys, girls, or boys and girls?**   ☐ Yes ☐ No ☐ Other

   If "Yes," **Which is easier?**
   ☐ Boys   ☐ Girls   ☐ Boys and Girls Together

5. **Does the age of the people matter?**   ☐ Yes ☐ No ☐ Other

   If "Yes," **Which is easier—older than you, younger than you, or the same age as you?**
   ☐ Older than you   ☐ Younger than you   ☐ Your age

6. **Does the size of the group make a difference?**   ☐ Yes ☐ No ☐ Other

   If "Yes," **Which is easier—big groups, small groups, or medium size groups?**
   ☐ Big   ☐ Small   ☐ Medium

7. **What do you think will happen when you are in** (give specifics of feared social situation)? _____

_____

_____

Interference

Okay, I want to know how much you feel this problem has messed things up in your life. That is, how much has it messed things up for you with friends, in school, or at home? How much does it stop you from doing things you would like to do? Tell me how much by using the Feelings Thermometer we discussed earlier, okay? If necessary, review the scale with the child. Show the child the Feelings Thermometer (found on the back cover of the Clinicial Manual) and obtain an overall rating of interference. Record the number corresponding to the child's anchor response, 0–8.

If clinical interference is indicated (a rating of 4 or greater), place a check mark in the diamond.

If all three diamonds are checked, consider Social Phobia (Social Anxiety Disorder) diagnosis and place a check mark in the star.

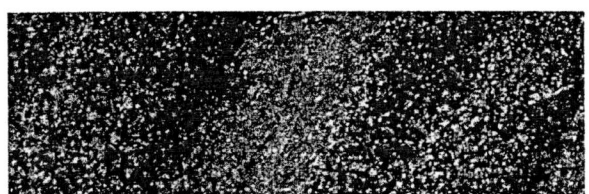

Specific Phobia

Initial Inquiry

Many kids (teenagers) **feel *really* scared and uncomfortable about certain, specific things, so scared and uncomfortable that they might want to stay away from these things. Some kids** (teenagers) **might also cry, or even have a temper tantrum, or get angry when they have to be around these things. Does this sound like you?**

☐ Yes ☐ No ☐ Other

If "Yes," place a check mark in the diamond.

◇ **CRITERION**

If "Yes" or "Other," **Can you tell me about that?** _____
_____ _____
_____

Make sure that the child is responding to fear of specific objects or situations. If unclear, ask, **Okay, but many kids might be scared of** (specific object or situation). **Is there anything that makes you really, really scared—more so than other kids your age?**

☐ Yes ☐ No ☐ Other

What is that? Can you tell me more about that? _____
_____
_____

Fear (Yes or No)

1a. **I have a list of some things** (see list following Question 2c) **that make some kids** (teenagers) **very, very nervous or scared. I'm going to give you a list of some things, and I would like you to tell me if you are really scared of these things—more afraid of them than most kids your ige are. First, just tell me "Yes" or "No," okay?**

Fear Ratings (0–8)

1b. For each situation in Question 1a to which the child responded "Yes," obtain fear ratings using the Feelings Thermometer.

Now, using the Feelings Thermometer, tell me how afraid you feel you are of these things that you said "Yes" to. Show the Feelings Thermometer and review, if necessary, to obtain the fear ratings.

For fear ratings of 4 or greater, place a check mark in the diamond

CRITERION

If no fears are reported in Question 1a or if all fear ratings in Question 1b are less than 2, skip to Panic Disorder (p. 27).

Avoidance (Yes or No)

1c. After obtaining the fear ratings, inquire for avoidance behavior for those items with a fear severity rating of 4 *(Some)* or greater. (If child is particularly sensitive, this inquiry may be stopped after one situation of avoidance is documented.)

Okay, you just told me how afraid you are of some things. Now I want you to tell me if you ever try to stay away from or avoid these things. For example, some kids might rate their fear of dogs at 8, meaning that they are very, very afraid, but if a dog was around they might still go up and pet it. But other kids who are very afraid of dogs can't go anywhere near a dog! So you see, I need to know how afraid you are, and also if you try to stay away from or avoid the things that you are scared of. Okay, so when you say that you are afraid of (phobic stimulus), **do you try to avoid** (phobic stimulus)?

If one or more "Yes" responses to Question 1c, place a check mark in the diamond.

CRITERION

	Fear Yes	Fear No	Fear Rating (0–8)	Avoidance/ Distress Yes	Avoidance/ Distress No	Interference (0–8)

Animal Type

Snakes, spiders, dogs, bees/insects
Specify: ☐ ☐ ☐ ☐ ☐ ☐

Natural Environment Type

High places, going up a ladder or a really tall building ☐ ☐ ☐ ☐ ☐ ☐

Thunderstorms or lightning ☐ ☐ ☐ ☐ ☐ ☐

Water, like in a swimming pool, lake, or ocean ☐ ☐ ☐ ☐ ☐ ☐

Darkness ☐ ☐ ☐ ☐ ☐ ☐

Blood-Injection or Injury Type

(Inquire and note for self and others)

Getting shots ☐ ☐ ☐ ☐ ☐ ☐

Having blood tests ☐ ☐ ☐ ☐ ☐ ☐

Seeing blood from a cut or scrape ☐ ☐ ☐ ☐ ☐ ☐

If "Yes," **Do you ever feel as if you are going to faint, or have you ever fainted, when you** (e.g., see blood, get a shot)?   ☐ Yes ☐ No ☐ Other

If "Yes" or "Other," **Tell me about that.** _____

_____

The interviewer should evaluate for vasovagal response and fainting characteristic of this specific phobia subtype. Inquire for triggers to fainting episodes.

Situational Type

Cars, planes, buses, or any other way of traveling
Specify: ☐ ☐ ☐ ☐ ☐ ☐

Elevators or small enclosed places ☐ ☐ ☐ ☐ ☐ ☐

Other Type

Loud noises (e.g., fireworks) ☐ ☐ ☐ ☐ ☐ ☐

Costumed characters ☐ ☐ ☐ ☐ ☐ ☐

Doctors or dentists ☐ ☐ ☐ ☐ ☐ ☐

	Fear		Fear Rating (0–8)	Avoidance/ Distress		Interference (0–8)
	Yes	No		Yes	No	
Vomiting	☐	☐	☐	☐	☐	☐
Choking	☐	☐	☐	☐	☐	☐
Catching a disease	☐	☐	☐	☐	☐	☐
Other (identified by the child)	☐	☐	☐	☐	☐	☐

Interference (0–8)

1d. For each identified specific phobia rated 4 *(Some)* or greater for fear, ask, **Now, when you say you're afraid of** (phobic stimulus), **are you so afraid that it bothers you and messes things up for you with friends or school or your family? Does it stop you from doing the things you would like to do? Tell me how much by using our thermometer.**

For any specific phobia endorsed with an interference rating of 4 or greater, place a check mark in the diamond.

2. **Have you been afraid of** (feared stimulus) **for at least six months?**   ☐ Yes ☐ No ☐ Other

If "Yes," to Question 2, place a check mark in the diamond.

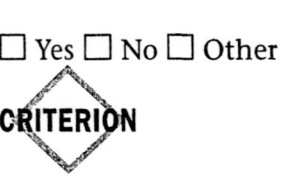

To meet diagnostic criteria for Specific Phobia, the child must have endorsed a fear of one or more objects or situations with a rating of 4 *(Some)* or greater; avoidance or endurance of the specific situation; and interference in normal routine, academic functioning, or social activities or relationships. The duration must be 6 months or longer.

If all five diamonds are endorsed, consider Specific Phobia diagnosis and place a check mark in the star.

DIAGNOSIS

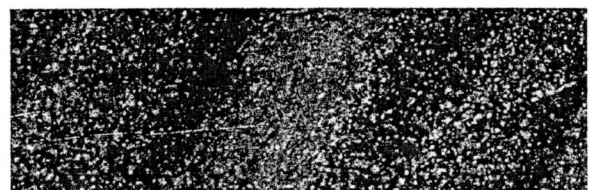

Panic Disorder

Initial Inquiry

1a. **Okay, we just talked about how sometimes people get scared because they are scared of a specific thing. For example, being scared of a dog or being scared of the dark. But sometimes some people feel really scared for no reason at all! They are not in a scary place and there is nothing scary around. But all of a sudden, out of the blue, they feel really scared and they don't know why. Has that ever happened to you?**

☐ Yes ☐ No ☐ Other

If "No," skip to Agoraphobia Without History of Panic Disorder (Question 1b on p. 33). Otherwise, continue.

1b. **What exactly happened? When did that happen? Where were you when you had these feelings? Was there anything to make you afraid then?** _____
_____
_____
_____

Make sure any "Yes" response is not simply caused by exposure to a certain situation or object (Specific Phobia), being the focus of attention (Social Phobia), being separated from parents (Separation Anxiety), and so on. If the child gives examples that are the result of another anxiety disorder or elaboration of the response to Question 1b suggests that the child does not seem to understand Question 1a, then ask Question 1c to reassess the presence of "unexpected" panic attacks, that is, those that do not occur immediately before or on exposure to a situation that almost always causes anxiety.

If the child does give examples of "unexpected" panic attacks, skip to Question 2.

Additional Probe

1c. **Okay, you just told me about getting scared when** (give specifics of situations mentioned by the child, e.g., being near a dog). **Now, at that time, you were probably scared of** (give specifics, e.g., the dog will bite you), **right? I'm talking about having that feeling at other times for no reason at all! That is, there is nothing to be scared of, but you feel scared anyway. Has that ever happened to you?**   ☐ Yes ☐ No ☐ Other

If "No," skip to Agoraphobia Without History of Panic Disorder (Question 1b on p. 33).

If "Yes," **When did that happen? Where were you when you had these feelings? Was there anything to make you afraid then?**

_____
_____
_____

If the child still gives an example that is a result of another anxiety disorder or if the child still does not understand the question, skip to Agoraphobia Without History of Panic Disorder (p. 33). Otherwise, continue.

2. **How many times have you had these feelings** (in place described by the child)?

If more than once, ask the child to elaborate. _____

_____

3a. **Have you ever had feelings like that in other places besides** (place described by the child)?   ☐ Yes ☐ No ☐ Other

If "No," skip to Question 4.

3b. **Where else has it happened?**

For each place the child mentions, obtain frequency and elaboration.
1. _____
2. _____
3. _____

Panic Attack Symptoms

In this section, inquire about symptoms only for panic attacks that occur unexpectedly in a variety of situations. Panic symptoms that are a result of another anxiety disorder (e.g., social or evaluative situations, specific objects, etc.) should not be rated here.

Inquire for the occurrence of each symptom that is typical of the most recent period of attacks. If a symptom is experienced only during some attacks (i.e., does *not* typically occur during an attack), enclose the child's response in parentheses.

Use the following inquiry and the list following Question 4b:

4a. **During these attacks, do you usually experience** (symptom)?

Record the child's responses in the "Symptom" column.

4b. If "Yes," **Is that feeling frightening or upsetting to you?** Record the child's responses in the "Distress" column.

	Symptom Yes	Symptom No	Distress Yes	Distress No
a. **Pounding heart, racing heart** (palpitations, tachycardia)	☐	☐	☐	☐
b. Sweating	☐	☐	☐	☐
c. Shaking or trembling	☐	☐	☐	☐
d. Trouble catching breath or feeling like you can't get enough air to breathe; feeling smothered	☐	☐	☐	☐
e. Feeling of choking	☐	☐	☐	☐
f. Chest pain or discomfort	☐	☐	☐	☐
g. Nausea or upset stomach; "butterflies"	☐	☐	☐	☐
h. Chills or hot flushes	☐	☐	☐	☐
i. Dizziness, lightheadedness, faintness, or unsteady feeling	☐	☐	☐	☐
j. Feeling like you're in a dream and things are not real; or like you're not really controlling your body and what you do	☐	☐	☐	☐
k. Numbing or tingling, like your hands and feet are falling asleep	☐	☐	☐	☐
l. Are you afraid that you're dying?	☐	☐	☐	☐
m. Are you afraid that you're going crazy?	☐	☐	☐	☐

	Symptom		Distress	
	Yes	No	Yes	No
n. Are you afraid that you're going to do something and you can't stop yourself?	☐	☐	☐	☐
o. Are you afraid that you're going to be sick and may even die?	☐	☐	☐	☐

If "Yes" to 4 or more symptoms (a–o), place a check mark in the circle.

SYMPTOM

5. **Have you ever had these feelings at least one time and then for the next four weeks were always scared that these feelings would come again?** (Use the ADIS for DSM–IV:C Calendar found at the back of the Interview Schedule to assist the child in establishing a time period.)

☐ Yes ☐ No ☐ Other

5a. **Did you worry that something might be really wrong or that maybe you wouldn't be able to stop yourself from doing something when you got these feelings? For example, did you think you'll just start running or screaming or that the feelings will never stop?**

☐ Yes ☐ No ☐ Other

If "Yes," **Tell me about that.** _____

_____

_____

5b. **Did these feelings stop you from doing things or cause you to do things differently?**

☐ Yes ☐ No ☐ Other

If "Yes," **Tell me about that.** _____

_____

_____

To meet the criteria for Panic Disorder the child must report recurrent, unexpected panic attacks at least one of which has been followed for a month by one or more symptoms.

If the child endorses symptoms consistent with unexpected panic attacks and responds "Yes" to any of Questions 5a–5b, place a check mark in the diamond.

CRITERION

Interference

Okay, I want to know how much you feel this problem has messed things up in your life. That is, how much has it messed things up for you with friends, in school, or at home? How much does it stop you from

Child's Rating

☐

doing things you would like to do? Tell me how much by using the Feelings Thermometer we discussed earlier, okay? If necessary, review the scale with the child. Show the child the Feelings Thermometer and obtain an overall rating of interference (record the number corresponding to the child's anchor response, 0–8).

If clinical interference is indicated (a rating of 4 or greater), place a check mark in the diamond.

CRITERION

If both diamonds are marked, continue. Otherwise, skip to Agoraphobia (p. 33).

Are there places that you don't like to go to because you are afraid that you will all of a sudden get scared and you wouldn't be able to get away or get help?

If "No," consider diagnosis of Panic Disorder Without Agoraphobia, mark the star below, and skip to Generalized Anxiety Disorder (p. 41). If "Yes," proceed to the next section for possible diagnosis of Panic Disorder With Agoraphobia.

Presence or absence of Agoraphobia (next section) must be assessed *before* it can be determined whether diagnosis will be Panic Disorder With Agoraphobia or Panic Disorder Without Agoraphobia.

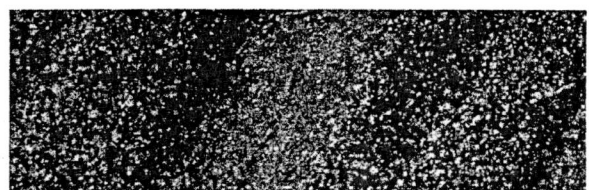

Agoraphobia (With or Without Panic Disorder)

Initial Inquiry

If Panic Disorder was diagnosed, ask Question 1a. If Panic Disorder has not been diagnosed, begin with Question 1b.

Panic Disorder With Agoraphobia

1a. **Okay, you just told me about the times that you suddenly got scared for no reason at all. Are there any places that you don't like to go to because you are afraid that you will all of a sudden get scared and you wouldn't be able to get away or get help?**

☐ Yes ☐ No ☐ Other

If "Yes" to Question 1a, place a check mark in the circle and skip to Question 2.

If "No," Panic Disorder Without Agoraphobia should have been diagnosed. Skip to Generalized Anxiety Disorder.

Agoraphobia Without History of Panic Disorder

1b. **Sometimes, some people don't want to go places, like a shopping mall or a crowded place. This is not because they're afraid of those places, but when they get there, they're afraid they might have an uncomfortable feeling in their body, like dizziness, or their heart might beat too fast, and then they won't be able to escape or get help. Have you felt that way?**

☐ Yes ☐ No ☐ Other

If "Yes" to Question 1b, place a check mark in the circle and continue.

If "No" to Question 1a or 1b, skip to Generalized Anxiety Disorder (p. 41).

If "Yes" to Question 1a or 1b, ask Question 2.

2. **What exactly happened? When did that happen? Where were you when that happened? Was there anything to make you afraid then? How many times has it happened? Has it happened any place else?**

_____
_____
_____
_____

If the child's response to Question 2 suggests that he or she did not understand Question 1a or 1b; or if the child's "Yes" response to Question 1a or 1b appears to be the result of exposure to a certain situation or object (Specific Phobia), being the focus of attention (Social Phobia), being separated from parents (Separation Anxiety), and so on; or if the child cites an obvious nonagoraphobic situation, then review Question 1a or 1b, emphasizing, rewording, and clarifying the specifics with which the child had difficulty. For example, for Question 1a, the child might not understand that he or she must be afraid "for no reason at all."

Continue only if the child reports experiencing a "clinically relevant" Agoraphobic experience to Question 2 after further probing. Otherwise, skip to Generalized Anxiety Disorder (p. 41).

Fear Ratings (0–8) and Avoidance (Yes or No)

3. **Okay, focusing on the place(s) that you just mentioned** (list specific situations provided by the child in Question 2), **I want to know how scared you feel when you are in those situations. I would like you to answer using the Feelings Thermometer I showed you before.**

For situations that the child endorses with a rating of 4 *(Some)* or greater, inquire about avoidance. Ask the child, **Do you try to stay away from** (situation) **or, if you have to be in these situations, does it make you very upset?**

Situations Mentioned by Child	Fear Rating (0–8)	Avoidance Yes	No
	☐	☐	☐
	☐	☐	☐
	☐	☐	☐
	☐	☐	☐
	☐	☐	☐

 If Panic Disorder has been diagnosed and Question 1a was answered yes, continue. If no diagnosis of Panic Disorder has been indicated and Question 1b was asked, skip to Questions 5a–5c.

Panic Disorder With Agoraphobia

For Questions 4a–4c, use the list following Question 4c.

Fear (Yes or No)

4a. **Okay, I'm now going to list some other places** (see list following Question 4c). **I would like you to tell me if you are afraid to go to any of these places because you think you might get scared for no reason and it would be hard to get away and get help or it would be embarrassing. First, just tell me "Yes" or "No."**

Fear Ratings (0–8)

4b. For those situations to which the child responded "Yes," obtain fear ratings using the Feelings Thermometer.

Now, using the Feelings Thermometer, tell me how afraid you feel.

Avoidance/Distress (Yes or No)

4c. For those situations that the child endorsed with a rating of 4 *(Some)* or greater, inquire for avoidance or enduring with distress.

Do you try to stay away from or avoid (specific situation)?

If one or more situations have a fear rating of 4 or greater and are avoided or endured with distress, place a check mark in the diamond, and skip to Questions 5a–5c.

	Fear		Fear Rating (0–8)	Avoidance/Distress	
	Yes	No		Yes	No
Classrooms	☐	☐	☐	☐	☐
School bus	☐	☐	☐	☐	☐
Cafeteria	☐	☐	☐	☐	☐
Other school situations Specify:	☐	☐	☐	☐	☐
Riding in a car	☐	☐	☐	☐	☐
Public transportation (e.g., bus, train)	☐	☐	☐	☐	☐
Crowds	☐	☐	☐	☐	☐
Waiting in line	☐	☐	☐	☐	☐
Doctor or dentist visit	☐	☐	☐	☐	☐
Restaurants	☐	☐	☐	☐	☐
Movie theaters or auditoriums	☐	☐	☐	☐	☐
Being at home alone	☐	☐	☐	☐	☐
Enclosed places: **Elevators** **Tunnels or small rooms**	☐	☐	☐	☐	☐
Open spaces (e.g., ballfields, parks, playground)	☐	☐	☐	☐	☐
Church or temple	☐	☐	☐	☐	☐
Being away from home	☐	☐	☐	☐	☐
Taking walks	☐	☐	☐	☐	☐
Stores or malls	☐	☐	☐	☐	☐
Camp (Specify type):	☐	☐	☐	☐	☐
Other (Specify)	☐	☐	☐	☐	☐

Agoraphobia Without History of Panic Disorder

For Questions 5a–5c, use the list following Question 5c.

Fear (Yes or No)

5a. **Okay, I'm now going to list some other places** (see list following Question 5c). **I would like you to tell me if you are scared to go to**

any of these places because you think you might get these feelings in your body and it would be hard to get away and get help or it would be embarrassing. First, just tell me "Yes" or "No."

Fear Ratings (0–8)

5b. For those situations to which the child responded "Yes," obtain fear ratings using the Feelings Thermometer.

Now, using the Feelings Thermometer, tell me how afraid you feel.

Avoidance (Yes or No)

5c. For those situations that the child endorsed with a fear rating of 4 or greater, inquire for avoidance.

Do you try to stay away from or avoid (specific situation)?

	Fear Yes	Fear No	Fear Rating (0–8)	Avoidance Yes	Avoidance No
Classrooms	☐	☐	☐	☐	☐
School bus	☐	☐	☐	☐	☐
Cafeteria	☐	☐	☐	☐	☐
Other school situations Specify:	☐	☐	☐	☐	☐
Riding in a car	☐	☐	☐	☐	☐
Public transportation (e.g., bus, train)	☐	☐	☐	☐	☐
Crowds	☐	☐	☐	☐	☐
Waiting in line	☐	☐	☐	☐	☐
Doctor or dentist visit	☐	☐	☐	☐	☐
Restaurants	☐	☐	☐	☐	☐
Movie theaters or auditoriums	☐	☐	☐	☐	☐
Being at home alone	☐	☐	☐	☐	☐
Enclosed places: Elevators Tunnels or small rooms	☐	☐	☐	☐	☐
Open spaces (e.g., ballfields, parks, playground)	☐	☐	☐	☐	☐
Church or temple	☐	☐	☐	☐	☐

	Fear		Fear Rating (0–8)	Avoidance	
	Yes	No		Yes	No
Being away from home	☐	☐	☐	☐	☐
Taking walks	☐	☐	☐	☐	☐
Stores or malls	☐	☐	☐	☐	☐
Camp (Specify type):	☐	☐	☐	☐	☐
Other (Specify)	☐	☐	☐	☐	☐

5d. If the child answered "Yes" to Question 1a and gives a fear rating of 4 *(Some)* or greater to at least one situation in Question 4a, then consider a diagnosis of Panic Disorder With Agoraphobia. Place a check mark in the appropriate diamond.

◇ **CRITERION**

If the child answered "Yes" to Question 1b and gives a rating of 4 *(Some)* or greater to at least one situation in Question 5b, then consider a diagnosis of Agoraphobia Without History of Panic Disorder. Place a check mark in the appropriate diamond. (In considering the above 2 questions, if only one situation was endorsed, rule out the possibility of specific Phobia.)

◇ **CRITERION**

Range of Activity

For those places you told me you are scared to go to (list places the child has mentioned), **tell me**

6a. **How long can you spend in one of those places before you get too scared?** (Assist the child in anchoring minutes versus hours to establish behavioral limits.) _____

_____

6b. **Are there times when those places do not make you scared?** If the child responds "Yes," ask, **What makes it less scary? When is it less scary?** _____

☐ Yes ☐ No ☐ Other

_____

6c. **Do you get scared only if the place is far away from home, or do you still get scared even if it is close to home?**

☐ Yes ☐ No ☐ Other

If "Yes," **Tell me about that.** _____

_____

6d. **Does it make it easier if someone goes with you?**   ☐ Yes ☐ No ☐ Other

If "Yes," Who? _____

Interference

Okay, I want to know how much this problem has messed things up in your life. That is, how much has it messed things up for you with friends, in school, or at home? How much does it stop you from doing things you would like to do? Tell me how much by using the Feelings Thermometer we discussed earlier, okay? If necessary, review the scale with the child. Show the child the Feelings Thermometer and obtain an overall rating of interference (record the number corresponding to the child's anchor response, 0–8).

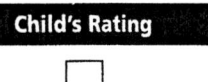

If clinical interference is indicated (a rating of 4 or greater), place a mark in the diamond.

The clinician should note whether the child meets diagnostic criteria for Panic Disorder With Agoraphobia or Agoraphobia Without History of Panic Disorder.

If the interference criteria is marked and the criteria is met for Panic Disorder With Agoraphobia (5d), mark the appropriate star.

If the interference criteria is marked and the criteria for Agoraphobia Without History of Panic Disorder is met (5e), mark the appropriate star.

Panic Disorder With Agoraphobia

Agoraphobia Without History of Panic Disorder   39 ■

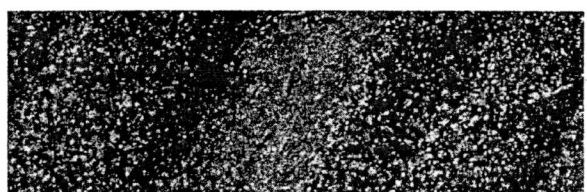

Generalized Anxiety Disorder

Initial Inquiry

Now I am going to ask you some questions that have to do with worrying, but first I want to make sure you know what I mean by worrying.

Give the child an opportunity to give his or her definition of worrying to determine whether the child understands the definition.

Clarify the meaning of worrying by saying, **Worrying is when you keep thinking about things over and over and it is hard to stop thinking about it. And the things you're thinking about are usually things that make you feel nervous or afraid. All kids worry, but sometimes kids worry so much it begins to bother them. Do you understand what I mean by worrying?**

1a. **Some children** (teenagers) **always seem to be worrying. They might worry about school and how well they are doing; or they might worry about things that might happen in the future; or they might worry about their friends, or family, or other things. Do you think you have been worried a lot about things like this lately?**   ☐ Yes ☐ No ☐ Other

If "Yes" to Question 1a, ask Question 1b.

1b. **What kinds of things do you worry about?** Ask the child to elaborate and record his or her responses. _____

_____

_____

Okay, now I want to ask you some specific questions about worrying.

Worry (Yes or No)

2a. Use the space below each general worry area in the list following Question 2c to record the specific content of the child's worry (including information obtained from Question 1b). Record the child's response (Yes or No) in the "Worry" column.

Okay, now I'd like you to tell me if you worry about certain things more than other kids (teenagers) **do. Just tell me "Yes" or "No." Do you worry about** (specific area) **more than other kids your age do?**

 If the child responds "No" to all the worry inquiries, skip to Obsessive–Compulsive Disorder (p. 45). Otherwise, continue with Question 2b.

Severity Ratings (0–8)

2b. For each worry area to which the child responded "Yes," inquire about excessiveness (severity rating).

Now, on our Feelings Thermometer, tell me how much do you feel you worry about (specific area)**?**

If one or more worry areas are endorsed with a severity rating of 4 *(Some)* or greater, place a check mark in the diamond.

Hard to Stop (Yes or No)

2c. For each worry area endorsed with a severity rating of 4 *(Some)* or greater, ask the child if it is hard to stop worrying (perceived control of symptom).

Is it hard to stop worrying about (specific worry area)**? For example, do you find yourself worrying about** (specific worry area) **when you are trying to do other things?**

Record the child's response (Yes or No) in the "Hard To Stop" column.

If the child reports the worry is hard to stop for one or more areas, place a check mark in the diamond.

 If no evidence of excessive or uncontrollable worry, skip to Obsessive–Compulsive Disorder (p. 45). Otherwise, continue.

	Worry		Severity Rating (0–8)	Hard To Stop	
	Yes	No		Yes	No
a. School (e.g., starting school, classwork, grades, homework)	☐	☐	☐	☐	☐
b. Performance (e.g., being good enough in things such as sports, dance, art)	☐	☐	☐	☐	☐
c. Social or Interpersonal (e.g., making friends, impressions, appearance)	☐	☐	☐	☐	☐
d. Little things (e.g., things that happened in the past, saying the wrong thing)	☐	☐	☐	☐	☐
e. Perfectionism (e.g., being on time, keeping schedules, never making mistakes)	☐	☐	☐	☐	☐
f. Health (self)	☐	☐	☐	☐	☐
g. Health (significant others)	☐	☐	☐	☐	☐
h. Family (divorce, finances)	☐	☐	☐	☐	☐
i. Things going on in the world (e.g., war; crime; community, local, and world affairs, floods, hurricanes, tornadoes)	☐	☐	☐	☐	☐
j. Other	☐	☐	☐	☐	☐

3a. **Do you usually worry about these things almost every day?** ☐ Yes ☐ No ☐ Other

If "Yes" to Question 3a, place a check mark in the diamond. **CRITERION**

3b. **Would you say you've been worried this way for at least six months?** ☐ Yes ☐ No ☐ Other

If "Yes" to Question 3b, place a check mark in the diamond. **CRITERION**

If no evidence of excessive or uncontrollable worry, skip to Obsessive–Compulsive Disorder (p. 45). Otherwise, inquire about physical symptoms.

4. **Okay,** (child's name)**, I was just asking you about different worries that you have. Now I am wondering if you get any physical feelings in your body when you worry.**

When you are worrying about (specific example)

    a. **Do you feel nervous and have trouble relaxing?**   ☐ Yes ☐ No ☐ Other

    b. **Do you get tired easily or feel tired all the time?**   ☐ Yes ☐ No ☐ Other

    c. **Do you have trouble paying attention or concentrating?**   ☐ Yes ☐ No ☐ Other

    d. **Do you get upset easily and sometimes get grouchy?**   ☐ Yes ☐ No ☐ Other

    e. **Do your muscles ache, like in your legs, arms, or neck?**   ☐ Yes ☐ No ☐ Other

    f. **Do you have trouble sleeping** (falling or staying asleep or have   ☐ Yes ☐ No ☐ Other
restless sleep)**?**

If "Yes" to one or more physical symptoms listed in Question 4, place a check mark in the diamond. ◇ **CRITERION**

To meet diagnostic criteria for Generalized Anxiety Disorder, the child must endorse excessive worry about a number of issues or situations, respond "Yes" to Questions 3a and 3b, report difficulty controlling the worry, endorse one physical symptom in Question 4, and report distress or impairment in functioning (interference) as indicated in the following section.

Interference

Okay, I want to know how much you feel this problem has messed things up in your life. How much has it messed things up for you with friends, in school, or at home? How much does it stop you from doing things you would like to do? Tell me how much by using the Feelings Thermometer we discussed earlier, okay? If necessary, review the scale with the child. Show the child the Feelings Thermometer and obtain an overall rating of interference (record the number corresponding to the child's anchor response, 0–8).

Child's Rating

☐

    If clinical interference is indicated (a rating of 4 or greater), place a check mark in the diamond. ◇ **CRITERION**

    If all six diamonds are checked, consider Generalized Anxiety Disorder diagnosis and place a check mark in the star.

Generalized Anxiety Disorder ★ **DIAGNOSIS**

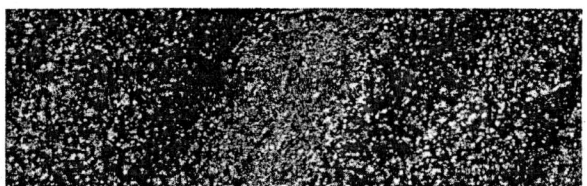

Obsessive–Compulsive Disorder

Obsessions

1a. **Now, I want to ask you more about worry, but this kind of worrying is different from what we were just talking about. Some people get thoughts or pictures in their minds that seem kind of silly or don't make sense. These thoughts can sometimes get pretty scary or upsetting, too. And they keep coming back over and over again, even though you want them to stop. These thoughts can be about all kinds of things, like thinking maybe you have germs on you, or that you forgot to lock the door at home, or that something bad is about to happen to your family. Do you ever get thoughts like that?** ☐ Yes ☐ No ☐ Other

If "No," skip to Question 1b.

If "Yes," **What kind of thoughts do you have?** _____

_____

_____

Additional Probe

1b. If the child did not appear to understand Question 1a, or if you are unsure, ask the following questions:

Do you ever get thoughts over and over about things like hurting yourself or someone else or bad things happening to someone? Or that you might get contaminated by germs or dirt? Or do you ever hear songs or sentences in your head over and over? ☐ Yes ☐ No ☐ Other

If "No" to any of these questions, skip to Compulsions (p. 48).

If there is any evidence of obsessive thoughts, place a check mark in the circle.

SYMPTOM

Ratings of Obsessions

In assessing for the clinical significance of obsessions, persistence is first assessed, then distress and resistance. Use the list following Question 2c for Questions 2a, 2b, and 2c.

Persistence Ratings (Yes or No)

2a. **Okay, now answer "Yes" only if you think about these things over and over again. That is, do you often think about** (obsession) **even when you don't want to?**

Record the child's responses (Yes or No) in the "Persistence" column.

If "Yes" to any obsession, place a check mark in the circle.

Distress Ratings (0–8)

2b. If "Yes" to any persistence query, obtain a rating for distress using the Feelings Thermometer.

How upset do you get when you think about (obsession)?

If any distress rating of 4 *(Some)* or greater, place a check mark in the circle.

Resistance—Trying To Stop (Yes or No)

2c. For any distress rating of 4 *(Some)* or greater, inquire about Resistance (Trying To Stop).

Do you try to stop the thought? For example, do you ignore it, do something else, or think about something else?

If "Yes" to any indication of resistance, place a check mark in the circle.

	Persistence Yes No	Distress Rating (0–8)	Resistance— Trying To Stop Yes No

Aggressive Obsessions

Do you get thoughts over and over about hurting yourself, hurting someone else, or wanting to break or throw things?

☐ ☐ ☐ ☐ ☐

Contamination

Do you get thoughts over and over about catching a disease or getting germs from touching things like doorknobs, things in bathrooms, or stuff that is sticky or gooey?

☐ ☐ ☐ ☐ ☐

Doubting

Do you tell yourself over and over that you didn't do a good job or that you weren't sure about something that you did or said?
For adolescents, ask,
Do you doubt how accurately or well you do things?

☐ ☐ ☐ ☐ ☐

Nonsensical Thoughts

Do you hear songs or sentences in your head over and over that you can't seem to stop?

☐ ☐ ☐ ☐ ☐

Do you have to repeat numbers, words, or letters over and over, even when you don't want to?

☐ ☐ ☐ ☐ ☐

Do you use special number, letters, or sayings so you won't feel nervous or scared?

☐ ☐ ☐ ☐ ☐

Hoarding or Saving

(*Note.* Distinguish from hobbies such as stamp or coin collecting.)
Do you save all sorts of things that you don't need, like old papers, bits of string, or other things, because you feel something bad could happen if you throw these things away?

☐ ☐ ☐ ☐ ☐

Religious or Satanic

Do you worry over and over about things like God or the devil? For example, do you worry very, very much about being good or saying your prayers perfectly so that you won't upset God?

☐ ☐ ☐ ☐ ☐

	Persistence Yes　　No	Distress Rating (0–8)	Resistance— Trying To Stop Yes　　No

Symmetry/Exactness

Do things have to be exactly in the right order or else you fear something terrible will happen? For example, do you have a special way of fixing things in your room, and, if so, when they are messed up, do you get very scared or nervous? Do things have to be "even," like if you touch your left leg, do you then have to touch your right leg?

☐　☐　　☐　　☐　☐

Miscellaneous

Are you bothered by gross thoughts, pictures of accidents or cut up bodies?
thoughts about hurting other people?
thoughts that something is wrong with your body, like being very afraid of gaining weight, being ugly, or being deformed?

☐　☐　　☐　　☐　☐

For older children: **Thoughts About Sex**

Are you bothered by thoughts or pictures in your mind about sex that have made you feel ashamed or uncomfortable?

☐　☐　　☐　　☐　☐

Other

Are there any other thoughts that you get over and over again that you can't seem to stop?

☐　☐　　☐　　☐　☐

About how much time each day do you spend thinking about (endorsed obsessions)? _____

Presence of one or more additional obsessions for more than 1 hour a day or endorsed with a rating of 4 *(Some)* or greater, place a check mark in the diamond.

CRITERION ◇

Compulsions

3a. **Some people have to do certain things over and over again, even though these things might seem silly. For example, they might have to turn the lights on and off over and over again, or count things, or wash their hands over and over. Do you have to do things over and over to stop yourself from feeling really uncomfortable or do**

☐ Yes ☐ No ☐ Other

you have to do things in a certain order or in a special way to stop yourself from feeling really uncomfortable?

If "No," skip to Question 3b.

If "Yes," place a check mark in the circle.

 SYMPTOM

If "Yes," **What kinds of things do you do?** _____

_____

_____

_____

Additional Probe

3b. If the child does not appear to understand the question, or if you are unsure, ask the following questions:

Do you have to use special numbers or have to do things a certain number of times? Or, do you count things over and over? Do you touch things in a special way or do you have to touch things a certain number of times? Do you have any special habits that you have to do before you go to bed or leave your house?

☐ Yes ☐ No ☐ Other

If "Yes" to any of these questions, place a check mark in the circle and continue.

SYMPTOM

Can you stop doing these things if you try?

☐ Yes ☐ No ☐ Other

Would it bother you if you couldn't do them?

☐ Yes ☐ No ☐ Other

If no evidence of compulsions and the child appeared to understand the questions, skip to Posttraumatic Stress Disorder (p. 53). Otherwise, continue.

Ratings of Compulsions

In assessing for compulsions, persistence is first assessed, then distress and resistance. Use the list following Question 4c for Questions 4a, 4b, and 4c.

Persistence (Yes or No)

4a. **Now, answer "Yes" only if you do things over and over each day. Do you have to do things such as** (compulsion) **over and over?**

Record the child's responses (Yes or No) in the "Persistence" column.

If "Yes" to any compulsive behavior, place a check mark in the circle.

Distress Ratings (0–8)

4b. If "Yes" to any persistence query, obtain a rating for distress using the Feelings Thermometer.

How upset do you get when you have to (compulsion)?

Resistance—Trying To Stop (Yes or No)

4c. For any distress rating of 4 *(Some)* or greater, inquire about Resistance (Trying To Stop).

Do you try to stop yourself from doing (compulsion)? **For example, do you try to ignore it or try to do something else?**

	Persistence		Distress Rating (0–8)	Resistance—Trying To Stop	
	Yes	No		Yes	No

Cleaning or Washing

Do you have to clean things over and over again? For example, do you have to wash your hands or shower (take a bath) **a lot during the day?**

☐ ☐ ☐ ☐ ☐

Checking

Do you have to check things over and over again? For example, do you check to make sure that the door is locked, check your toys or school books, check that you didn't make a mistake or do something bad, check that nothing terrible will happen to you or to your family, or check that your body is okay?

☐ ☐ ☐ ☐ ☐

Counting

Do you count things over and over again or have to do things over and over a special number of times?

☐ ☐ ☐ ☐ ☐

Hoarding or Collecting

Do you have to save things or do you find it hard to throw away stuff like old papers, string, and so on because you think you might need them again?

☐ ☐ ☐ ☐ ☐

	Persistence Yes No	Distress Rating (0–8)	Resistance— Trying To Stop Yes No

Repeating

Do you have to do things over and over again like your homework papers, going in and out of doorways, or getting up and down out of chairs? ☐ ☐ ☐ ☐ ☐

Do you have to read things over and over? Do you erase and rewrite things over and over? ☐ ☐ ☐ ☐ ☐

Ordering or Arranging

Do you line things up in a certain way, like your books and toys, or else you get very upset? ☐ ☐ ☐ ☐ ☐

Do things have to be "even" all the time, like if you touch your left leg, do you then have to touch your right leg? ☐ ☐ ☐ ☐ ☐

Miscellaneous Rituals

Do you have to

touch, tap, or rub things in a special way? ☐ ☐ ☐ ☐ ☐

always ask if you did the right thing or did something okay? ☐ ☐ ☐ ☐ ☐

have to ask the same question over and over? ☐ ☐ ☐ ☐ ☐

feel like you have to "tell on yourself"? ☐ ☐ ☐ ☐ ☐

*keep pulling your hair out (trichotillomania)? ☐ ☐ ☐ ☐ ☐

keep saying the same words, prayers, or sentences in your head over and over? ☐ ☐ ☐ ☐ ☐

*eat or drink things in a special order? Only eat certain foods? ☐ ☐ ☐ ☐ ☐

*Note. If such symptoms are endorsed, further evaluation is necessary for accurate differential diagnosis from other Axis I disorders.

How much time do you think you spend each day doing the things you have told me about? _____

If "Yes" to any compulsive behavior, place a check mark in the circle.

SYMPTOM

Presence of one or more compulsive behaviors for more than 1 hour a day with distress rated at 4 *(Some)* or greater, place a check mark in the diamond.

Diagnoses of Obsessive–Compulsive Disorder requires the presence of persistent obsessions, compulsions, or both (more than 1 hour each day) that are repetitive and difficult to control. In addition, the symptoms must cause marked distress or cause significant interference in functioning, as indicated in the following section. Recognition by the child that the symptoms are excessive or unreasonable is not necessary to make the diagnosis in children.

If no evidence of Obsessions or Compulsions is obtained, skip to Posttraumatic Stress Disorder (p. 53). Otherwise, continue.

Interference

Okay, I want to know how much you feel this problem (specify obsessive thoughts or compulsive behaviors mentioned by the child) **has messed things up in your life. That is, how much has it messed things up for you with friends, in school, or at home? How much does it stop you from doing things you would like to do? Tell me how much by using the Feelings Thermometer we discussed earlier, okay?** If necessary, review the scale with the child. Show the child the Feelings Thermometer and obtain an overall rating of interference (record the number corresponding to the child's anchor response, 0–8).

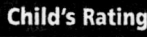

If clinical interference is indicated (a rating of 4 or greater), place a check mark in the diamond.

If two or more diamonds are checked, consider Obsessive–Compulsive Disorder diagnosis and place a check mark in the star.

Obsessive–Compulsive Disorder

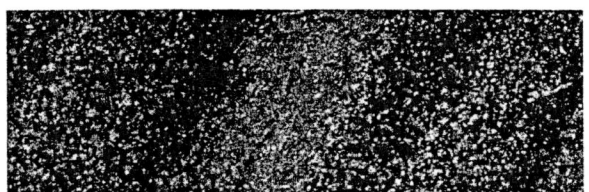

Posttraumatic Stress Disorder (PTSD)/Acute Stress Disorder

Initial Inquiry

Okay, (child's name), **now I want to ask you some questions that are a little bit different. These things might be hard to talk about, but it's important that I ask you these questions. It's very important that you tell me now if any of these things ever happened to you. I'm going to ask you whether anything happened to you that was really frightening or upsetting and you felt like there was nothing you could do to stop it from happening. Okay?**

Note. For any "Yes" response, ensure that the event was extremely distressful or upsetting to the child and that the child's physical integrity was threatened. It is important that the child perceived the event as traumatic to qualify for the diagnosis.

By *DSM–IV* definition, the person must have experienced, witnessed, or been confronted with (an) event(s) that involved actual or threatened death, injury, or threat to the physical integrity of self or others; the person's response must involve intense fear, helplessness, horror, or, in children, disorganized or agitated behavior.

Traumatic Event

1. **Have you ever had anything really terrible or upsetting happen to you, like being very sick or badly hurt?** ☐ Yes ☐ No ☐ Other

   If "Yes," place a check mark in the circle. **SYMPTOM**

   If "Yes," **What happened?** _____

   _____

2. **Have you ever seen anyone die or badly hurt?**   □ Yes □ No □ Other

   If "Yes," place a check mark in the circle.

   If "Yes," **What happened?** _____
   _____

   SYMPTOM

3. **Have you ever been in a really bad accident or fire where you could have died?**   □ Yes □ No □ Other

   If "Yes," place a check mark in the circle.

   If "Yes," **What happened?** _____
   _____

   SYMPTOM

4. **Have you ever been in anything like a really bad hurricane, flood, or earthquake or had a tornado near where you lived?**   □ Yes □ No □ Other

   If "Yes," place a check mark in the circle.

   If "Yes," **What happened?** _____
   _____

   SYMPTOM

5. **Has anyone ever robbed you or attacked you?**   □ Yes □ No □ Other

   If "Yes," place a check mark in the circle.

   If "Yes," **What happened?** _____
   _____

   SYMPTOM

6. **Has anyone ever touched you on parts of your body that you really didn't want them to touch?**   □ Yes □ No □ Other

   If "Yes," place a check mark in the circle.

   If "Yes," **What happened?** _____
   _____

   SYMPTOM

7. **Has anyone ever made you touch them in places that you didn't want to?**   □ Yes □ No □ Other

   If "Yes," place a check mark in the circle.

   If "Yes," **What happened?** _____
   _____

   SYMPTOM

8. **Has anyone ever hit you over and over or hurt you very badly?** ☐ Yes ☐ No ☐ Other

   If "Yes," place a check mark in the circle.

   SYMPTOM

   If "Yes," **What happened?** _____

   _____

9. **Is there anything else that someone has done to you, or makes you do, that you don't like?** ☐ Yes ☐ No ☐ Other

   If "Yes," place a check mark in the circle.

   SYMPTOM

   If "Yes," **What happened?** _____

   _____

   If one or more circles for Questions 1–9 have been checked, place a check mark in the diamond and continue.

   CRITERION

10. **How long ago did** (PTSD event) **happen?** _____

    PTSD event specified by the child: _____

    If response to Question 10 is more than 1 month, place a mark in the diamond and continue. Otherwise, skip to Affective Disorders: Dysthymia (p. 59).

    CRITERION

    Note. If event occurred less than 1 month ago consider diagnosis of Acute Stress Disorder.

PTSD Symptoms

Reexperiencing Symptoms

11. **Do you have a lot of thoughts that you don't want to have about** (PTSD event)**?** ☐ Yes ☐ No ☐ Other

    For young children, ask, **Do you ever play or draw pictures about** (PTSD event)**?**

    If "Yes," place a check mark in the circle.

    SYMPTOM

12. **Do you have a lot of bad dreams about** (PTSD event)**?** ☐ Yes ☐ No ☐ Other

    If "Yes," place a check mark in the circle.

    SYMPTOM

13. **Do you sometimes feel that** (PTSD event) **is about to happen again?**

☐ Yes ☐ No ☐ Other

If "Yes," place a check mark in the circle.

SYMPTOM

14. **When things remind you of** (PTSD event)**, do you get very upset?**

☐ Yes ☐ No ☐ Other

If "Yes," place a check mark in the circle.

SYMPTOM

15. **When things remind you of** (PTSD event)**, do you get uncomfortable feelings in your body? For example, does your heart beat real fast, or do you sweat or shake?**

☐ Yes ☐ No ☐ Other

If "Yes," place a check mark in the circle.

SYMPTOM

If one or more circles for Questions 11–15 have been checked, place a check mark in the diamond. Otherwise, skip to Affective Disorders (p. 59).

CRITERION

Avoidance Symptoms

16. **Do you try very hard not to think about** (PTSD event)**?**

☐ Yes ☐ No ☐ Other

If "Yes," place a check mark in the circle.

SYMPTOM

17. **Do you try to stay away from things that remind you of** (PTSD event)**?**

☐ Yes ☐ No ☐ Other

If "Yes," place a check mark in the circle.

SYMPTOM

18. **Are there some things about** (PTSD event) **that you can't remember?**

☐ Yes ☐ No ☐ Other

If "Yes," place a check mark in the circle.

SYMPTOM

19. **Since** (PTSD event)**, have you stopped doing things that you used to enjoy, such as playing games, going on outings, or doing hobbies?**

☐ Yes ☐ No ☐ Other

If "Yes," place a check mark in the circle.

SYMPTOM

20. **Have you become less interested in seeing friends since** (PTSD event)**?**

☐ Yes ☐ No ☐ Other

If "Yes," place a check mark in the circle.

SYMPTOM

21. **Since** (PTSD event), **has it become difficult for you to show other people how you feel? For example, are you hiding your feelings and keeping them to yourself?**

    If "Yes," place a check mark in the circle.

    ☐ Yes ☐ No ☐ Other

    SYMPTOM

22. **Do you think that when you grow up, you will be able to do all of the things that you would like to do, such as going to college, getting married or getting a job, having children or things like that?**

    If "No," place a check mark in the circle.

    ☐ Yes ☐ No ☐ Other

    SYMPTOM

23. **Since** (PTSD event), **are you doing some things now that you haven't done since you were a little kid, like maybe wetting your pants or bed, sucking your thumb, or always wanting to be with your mom or dad?**

    If "Yes," place a check mark in the circle.

    ☐ Yes ☐ No ☐ Other

    SYMPTOM

If three or more circles for Questions 16–23 have been checked, place a check mark in the diamond. Otherwise, skip to Affective Disorders (p. 59).

CRITERION

Hyperarousal Symptoms

Have you had any of these problems since (PTSD event)?

24a. **Trouble sleeping**

    If "Yes," place a check mark in the circle.

    ☐ Yes ☐ No ☐ Other

    SYMPTOM

24b. **Losing your temper**

    If "Yes," place a check mark in the circle.

    ☐ Yes ☐ No ☐ Other

    SYMPTOM

24c. **Having a hard time paying attention**

    If "Yes," place a check mark in the circle.

    ☐ Yes ☐ No ☐ Other

    SYMPTOM

24d. **Being on the "look out" a lot so you will be ready if something bad happens**

    If "Yes," place a check mark in the circle.

    ☐ Yes ☐ No ☐ Other

    SYMPTOM

24e. When things happen by surprise or all of a sudden, like hearing a loud noise that you didn't expect, does it make you "jump"? (The interviewer should display startle response.)

If "Yes," place a check mark in the circle.

If two or more circles for Questions 24a–24e have been checked, place a check mark in the diamond. Otherwise, skip to Affective Disorders (p. 59).

In order to meet diagnostic criteria for Posttraumatic Disorder (PTSD), the child must answer "Yes" to at least one of Questions 1–9, "Yes" to one of Questions 11–15, "Yes" to three of Questions 16–23, and "Yes" to two of Questions 24a–24e. In addition, symptoms must be present for more than 1 month and interference in functioning (a rating of 4 or greater) must be evident. If less than 1 month since traumatic event, consider Acute Stress Disorder.

Interference

Okay, I want to know how much you feel this problem has messed things up in your life. That is, how much has it messed things up for you with friends, in school, or at home? How much does it stop you from doing things you would like to do? Tell me how much by using the Feelings Thermometer we discussed earlier, okay? If necessary, review the scale with the child. Show the child the Feelings Thermometer and obtain an overall rating of interference (record the number corresponding to the child's anchor response, 0–8).

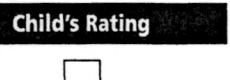

If clinical interference is indicated, place a check mark in the diamond.

If all six diamonds are checked, consider Posttraumatic Stress Disorder diagnosis and place a check mark in the star.

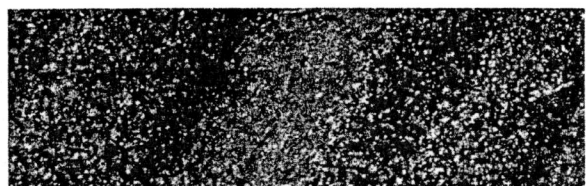

Affective Disorders: Dysthymia

Initial Inquiry

1a. **Have you ever had a whole year where you felt sad more days than you felt good?** ☐ Yes ☐ No ☐ Other

1b. **Have you been feeling sad more days than you feel good this past year?** ☐ Yes ☐ No ☐ Other

If "Yes" to Question 1a or 1b, place a check mark in the diamond and continue. **CRITERION**

1c. **During that** (this) **year, was there ever a two-month period of time when you actually felt good *more* days than you felt bad? For example, did you feel good during the summer?** ☐ Yes ☐ No ☐ Other

If the child responds "Yes" to Question 1c, then Dysthymia may not be present. Continue.

2. **During this time, did you also have trouble eating or sleeping?** ☐ Yes ☐ No ☐ Other

If "Yes," place a check mark in the circle. **SYMPTOM**

3. **During this time did you also have trouble keeping your mind on things?** ☐ Yes ☐ No ☐ Other

If "Yes," place a check mark in the circle. **SYMPTOM**

4. **Did you feel very tired and not want to do much?** ☐ Yes ☐ No ☐ Other

If "Yes," place a check mark in the circle. **SYMPTOM**

If one or more circles for Questions 2–4 have been checked, place a check mark in the diamond and continue. **CRITERION**

Okay, now I am going to tell you about things that happen to some people when they feel really sad. I want to find out if these things happened to you when you felt sad like that. It could be either something that you yourself noticed or maybe somebody else noticed. For example, sometimes when people are really sad, they have trouble eating. So I am going to ask you if you have trouble eating when you feel sad. It could be that either you noticed that you had trouble eating or somebody, like maybe your mother, told you. Do you understand?

Okay, now answer "Yes" only if the things I ask you happened during that year that you felt sad.

5a. **Ate more than usual**   ☐ Yes ☐ No ☐ Other

5b. **Ate less than usual**   ☐ Yes ☐ No ☐ Other

Count any "Yes" response to Questions 5a and 5b as one symptom only and place a check mark in the circle.   **SYMPTOM**

6a. **Had trouble sleeping**   ☐ Yes ☐ No ☐ Other

6b. **Slept a lot more than usual**   ☐ Yes ☐ No ☐ Other

Count any "Yes" response to Questions 6a and 6b as one symptom only and place a check mark in the circle.   **SYMPTOM**

7. **Felt really tired or had no energy**   ☐ Yes ☐ No ☐ Other

If "Yes," place a check mark in the circle.   **SYMPTOM**

8. **Felt that you were no good**   ☐ Yes ☐ No ☐ Other

If "Yes," place a check mark in the circle.   **SYMPTOM**

9. For children, ask, **Had trouble keeping your mind on things or making up your mind**   ☐ Yes ☐ No ☐ Other

For adolescents, ask, **Had trouble making decisions**

If "Yes," place a check mark in the circle.   **SYMPTOM**

10. For children, ask, **Felt that things would never work out right**   ☐ Yes ☐ No ☐ Other

For adolescents, ask, **Felt that things were hopeless**

If "Yes," place a check mark in the circle.   **SYMPTOM**

If two or more circles for Questions 5–10 have been checked, place a check mark in the diamond. Otherwise, skip to Major Depressive Disorder (p. 63).

CRITERION

11. **Are you feeling sad like that now? When was the last time you felt sad like that? How long have you been feeling this way?** (Assess for current dysthymia.) _____

_____

_____

If the child reports the presence of at least two of the symptoms in Questions 5–10, consider Dysthymia diagnosis. Whether or not the child meets criteria for Dysthymia, all children should be assessed for Major Depressive Disorder.

Interference

Okay, I want to know how much you feel this problem has messed things up in your life. That is, how much has it messed things up for you with friends, in school, or at home? How much does it stop you from doing things you would like to do? Tell me how much by using the Feelings Thermometer we discussed earlier, okay? If necessary, review the scale with the child. Show the child the Feelings Thermometer and obtain an overall rating of interference (record the number corresponding to the child's anchor response, 0–8).

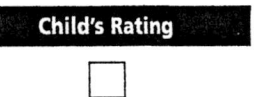

If clinical interference is indicated (a rating of 4 or greater), place a check mark in the diamond.

CRITERION

If all four diamonds are checked, consider Dysthymia diagnosis and place a check mark in the star.

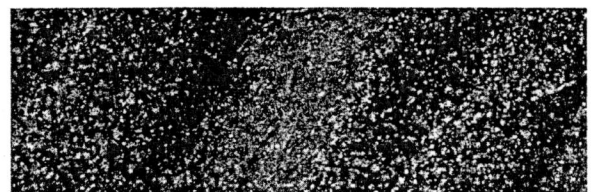

Affective Disorders: Major Depressive Disorder

Initial Inquiry

Now, I want to ask you again about sad feelings, but this time it's about feeling even more sad than we just talked about. Do you know what it means to be depressed?

Determine whether the child understands the meaning of *depressed*.

Clarify the meaning of *depressed* by saying, **Depressed is a feeling that some people have when they are feeling very, very sad. Now it's not like the feeling we just talked about or the feeling someone gets when a pet dies or a good friend moves away. It's a lot worse. I'm talking about feeling so sad that they just can't seem to have fun anymore and they don't feel that good things are ever going to happen to them again. Also, a lot of times they feel very tired and they don't want to do much.**

Do you understand what I mean now by "feeling depressed"? Be certain that the child understands the meaning.

1a. **Okay,** (child's name), **have you ever felt depressed?**   ☐ Yes ☐ No ☐ Other

   If "No," the presence of specific symptoms (4a–11d) may be probed.

1b. **If "yes" tell me about that.** _____

   _____

   _____

   If the child responds "Yes" to Question 1a and reports an episode that is clinical in nature in Question 1b, then place a check mark in the diamond and continue. If the child

CRITERION

responds "Yes" to Question 1a but reports an episode that is nonclinical in nature in Question 1b, then probe further to determine whether the child ever experienced clinically significant depressive episodes.

2. **Have you ever felt that way for more than one day?**   ☐ Yes ☐ No ☐ Other

If "No," skip to Externalizing Disorders (p. 67). Otherwise, continue.

3a. **Have you ever felt that way every day for at least two weeks?**   ☐ Yes ☐ No ☐ Other

3b. **Have you been feeling depressed almost every day for these past two weeks?**   ☐ Yes ☐ No ☐ Other

If "Yes" to Question 3a or 3b, inquire whether there was a legitimate reason for sadness (death in family, etc.). If inquiry shows that depression was limited to those instances in which there was a legitimate reason and was not longer or more severe than would be expected, code as "Other" and skip to Externalizing Disorders (p. 67). Otherwise, place a check mark in the diamond and continue.

CRITERION

If "No" to Question 3a or 3b, skip to Externalizing Disorders (p. 67).

3c. **Are you feeling sad like that now? When was the last time you felt sad like that? How long have you been feeling this way?** _____

_____

If necessary, use the ADIS for DSM–IV:C Calendar found at the back of the interview schedule to illustrate a 2-week period.

Depressive Symptoms

Okay, now I am going to tell you about things that happen to some people when they feel depressed. I want to find out if these things happen to you when you feel depressed. It could be either something that you yourself noticed or maybe somebody else noticed. For example, sometimes when people are depressed they have trouble eating so I am going to ask you if you have trouble eating when you feel like that. So it could be that either you noticed that you had trouble eating or somebody, like maybe your mother, told you. Do you understand?

Okay, now I only want you to answer "Yes" if the things I asked you happened almost every day for at least two weeks. For example, if you had trouble eating just one day, you would answer "No" because it was not every day. But if it was almost every day, then you would answer "Yes." (Point to almost every day during a 2-week period on the calendar. If necessary, elaborate with further examples.)

4a. **Ate more than usual**   ☐ Yes ☐ No ☐ Other

4b. **Ate less than usual**   ☐ Yes ☐ No ☐ Other

4c. **Gained weight**   ☐ Yes ☐ No ☐ Other

4d. **Lost weight**   ☐ Yes ☐ No ☐ Other

Count any "Yes" response to Questions 4a–4d as one symptom only and place check mark in circle.   **SYMPTOM**

5a. **Had trouble sleeping**   ☐ Yes ☐ No ☐ Other

5b. **Slept a lot more than usual**   ☐ Yes ☐ No ☐ Other

Count any "Yes" response to Questions 5a and 5b as one symptom only and place a check mark in the circle.   **SYMPTOM**

6a. **Had trouble sitting still**   ☐ Yes ☐ No ☐ Other

6b. **Moved very, very slowly**   ☐ Yes ☐ No ☐ Other

Count any "Yes" response to Questions 6a and 6b as one symptom only and place a check mark in the circle.   **SYMPTOM**

7. **Things were not fun**   ☐ Yes ☐ No ☐ Other

If "Yes," place a check mark in the circle.   **SYMPTOM**

8. **Felt really tired or had no energy**   ☐ Yes ☐ No ☐ Other

If "Yes," place a check mark in the circle.   **SYMPTOM**

9. **Felt that you were no good or blamed yourself for lots of bad things**   ☐ Yes ☐ No ☐ Other

If "Yes," place a check mark in the circle.   **SYMPTOM**

10. **Had trouble thinking or keeping your mind on things**   ☐ Yes ☐ No ☐ Other

If "Yes," place a check mark in the circle.   **SYMPTOM**

11a. Thought a lot about death or dying ☐ Yes ☐ No ☐ Other

11b. Thought about killing yourself ☐ Yes ☐ No ☐ Other

Okay, you just answered whether some things happened almost every day for two weeks when you felt really sad. Now, I am going to ask you a couple more things, and I just want to know if it ever happened at all, even just once.

11c. Thought of a way to try to kill yourself ☐ Yes ☐ No ☐ Other

11d. Tried to kill yourself ☐ Yes ☐ No ☐ Other

Count any "Yes" response to Questions 11a–11d as one symptom only and place a check mark in the circle.

SYMPTOM

If the child responds "Yes" to Question 11a, 11b, 11c, or 11d, the interviewer should obtain further details and assess the current risk of harm to self or others. Inquire about specifics of plan, time of occurrence, frequency of such thoughts, details of the attempt, current absence or presence of ideation, and so on, and take appropriate preventative action.

Diagnosis of Major Depressive Disorder requires five "Yes" responses to Questions 4–11. Also, the symptoms must occur together nearly every day for at least 2 weeks. If five or more circles are checked, place a check mark in the diamond.

CRITERION

Interference

Okay, I want to know how much you feel this problem has messed things up in your life. That is, how much has it messed things up for you with friends, in school, or at home? How much does it stop you from doing things you would like to do? Tell me how much by using the Feelings Thermometer we discussed earlier, okay? If necessary, review the scale with the child. Show the child the Feelings Thermometer and obtain an overall rating of interference (record the number corresponding to the child's anchor response, 0–8).

Child's Rating

☐

If clinical interference is indicated (a rating of 4 or greater), place a check mark in the diamond.

CRITERION

If all four diamonds are checked, consider Major Depressive diagnosis and place a check mark in the star.

Major Depressive Disorder **DIAGNOSIS**

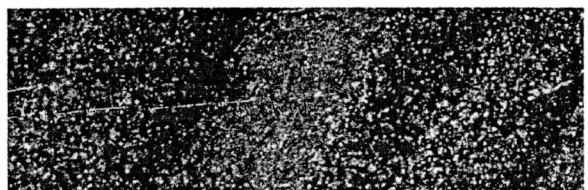

Externalizing Disorders

Up until now all of the questions I've asked you have had to do with feeling scared, nervous, worried, or sad. But now, I'll be asking you about things you might do or ways you might act that might make it hard for you at school, with friends, or at home.

Attention-Deficit/Hyperactivity Disorder (ADHD)

Attention Deficit

1. **Do you often make little mistakes, like on school work, or chores, or other things that you do?**   ☐ Yes ☐ No ☐ Other

   If "Yes," place a check mark in the circle.   **SYMPTOM**

2. For younger children, ask, **When you are supposed to be paying attention to one thing, do you find yourself paying attention to other things?**   ☐ Yes ☐ No ☐ Other

   For adolescents, ask, **Are you easily distracted?**

   If "Yes," place a check mark in the circle.   **SYMPTOM**

3. **Do people often complain that you don't listen or pay attention?**   ☐ Yes ☐ No ☐ Other

   If "Yes," place a check mark in the circle.   **SYMPTOM**

4. **Do you find that you just can't finish things that others ask you to do, such as chores, homework, and so forth?**   ☐ Yes ☐ No ☐ Other

   If "Yes," place a check mark in the circle.   **SYMPTOM**

 If "Yes" to any of Questions 1–4, continue. Otherwise, skip to Hyperactivity–Impulsivity (p. 69).

5. **Is it hard to keep your schoolwork or other things in order** (organized)?

☐ Yes ☐ No ☐ Other

If "Yes," place a check mark in the circle.

SYMPTOM

6a. **Do you dislike doing your schoolwork or homework because it's hard to keep your mind on things like that?**

☐ Yes ☐ No ☐ Other

6b. **Do you not do your schoolwork or homework because it's hard to keep your mind on things like that?**

☐ Yes ☐ No ☐ Other

Count any "Yes" response to Questions 6a and 6b as one symptom and place a check mark in the circle.

SYMPTOM

If three or more circles for Questions 1–6 have been checked, continue. Otherwise, skip to Hyperactivity–Impulsivity (p. 69).

7. **Do you often lose things that you need, such as school books, pencils, toys, and so on?**

☐ Yes ☐ No ☐ Other

If "Yes," place a check mark in the circle.

SYMPTOM

8. **Do you have trouble concentrating on things when there's noise or other things going on around you?**

☐ Yes ☐ No ☐ Other

If "Yes," place a check mark in the circle.

SYMPTOM

9. **Do you often lose your place or forget what you were doing?**

☐ Yes ☐ No ☐ Other

If "Yes," place a check mark in the circle.

SYMPTOM

If six or more circles for Questions 1–9 have been checked, place a check mark in the diamond and continue. Otherwise skip to Hyperactivity–Impulsivity (p. 69).

CRITERION

10. **How old were you when you started** (list items to which the child responded "Yes")? _____

_____

_____

If response is before age 7, place a check mark in the diamond.

CRITERION

Hyperactivity–Impulsivity

1. **Do you usually have a lot of trouble staying in your seat?**   ☐ Yes ☐ No ☐ Other

   If "Yes," place a check mark in the circle.   SYMPTOM

2. For children, ask, **Do you get yelled at because you run around a lot or climb on things, such as the furniture?**   ☐ Yes ☐ No ☐ Other

   For adolescents, ask, **Do you often feel restless, like you need to keep moving or doing something?**

   If "Yes," place a check mark in the circle.   SYMPTOM

3. For children, ask, **Do you have trouble playing quietly?**   ☐ Yes ☐ No ☐ Other

   For adolescents, ask, **Do you have trouble sitting and doing things quietly by yourself?**

   If "Yes," place a check mark in the circle.   SYMPTOM

4. For children, ask, **Are you almost always moving your hands and feet?**

   For adolescents, ask, **Do you often feel restless?**

   If "Yes," place a check mark in the circle.   SYMPTOM

If one or more circles for Questions 1–4 are checked, continue. Otherwise, skip to Question 11a (p. 70).

5. **Do you always seem to be doing things? For example, do you go from one activity to another all day?**   ☐ Yes ☐ No ☐ Other

   If "Yes," place a check mark in the circle.   SYMPTOM

6. **Do people tell you that you talk too much?**   ☐ Yes ☐ No ☐ Other

   If "Yes," place a check mark in the circle.   SYMPTOM

If three or more circles for Questions 1–6 are checked, continue. Otherwise, skip to Screening Questions (p. 73).

7. **Do you usually answer a question before the person is done asking it?**   ☐ Yes ☐ No ☐ Other

   If "Yes," place a check mark in the circle.   SYMPTOM

8. **Is it hard to wait for your turn in games or in groups?** □ Yes □ No □ Other

If "Yes," place a check mark in the circle.

9. **Do people tell you that you "butt into" things too much?** □ Yes □ No □ Other

If "Yes," place a check mark in the circle.

If six or more circles for Questions 1–9 have been checked, place a check mark in the diamond and continue. If the diamond for Attention Deficit has been checked but not the diamond for Hyperactivity–Impulsivity, continue. Otherwise skip to Screening Questions (p. 73).

10. **How old were you when you started** (list some items to which the child responded "Yes")? _____
_____
_____

If response is below age 7, place a check mark in the diamond.

11a. **Do you** (list some items to which the child responded "Yes") **in school?** □ Yes □ No □ Other

If "Yes," place a check mark in the circle.

11b. **Do you** (list some items to which the child responded "Yes") **at home?** □ Yes □ No □ Other

If "Yes," place a check mark in the circle.

11c. **Do you** (list some items to which the child responded "Yes") **with friends?** □ Yes □ No □ Other

If "Yes," place a check mark in the circle.

If two or more circles for Questions 11a–11c have been checked, place a check mark in the diamond and continue. Otherwise, skip to Screening Questions (p. 73).

Interference

Okay, I want to know your feelings about how much this problem has messed things up in your life. That is, how much has it messed things up for you with friends, in school, or at home? How much does it stop you

□

from doing things you would like to do? Tell me how much by using the thermometer we discussed earlier, okay? If necessary, review the scale with the child. Show the child the Feelings Thermometer and obtain an overall rating of interference (record the number corresponding to the child's anchor response, 0–8).

If clinical interference is indicated (a rating of 4 or greater), place a check mark in the diamond.

 **CRITERION**

To meet criteria for a diagnosis of ADHD, the child must respond "Yes" to at least six of Questions 1–9 in the Attention Deficit section and "Yes" to at least six of Questions 1–9 in the Hyperactivity–Impulsivity section. Also, the child must have indicated that the problem has been going on for at least 6 months, began before age 7, and occurs in more than one setting.

Specific ADHD subtypes might apply if criteria are met for only Attention Deficit or Hyperactivity–Impulsivity.

If all diamonds in Attention Deficit but none in Hyperactivity–Impulsivity are checked, consider ADHD Predominantly Inattentive Type (Attention Deficit) diagnosis and place a check mark in the corresponding star.

If no diamonds in Attention Deficit and all diamonds in Hyperactivity–Impulsivity are checked, consider ADHD Predominantly Hyperactive–Impulsive Type (Hyperactivity–Impulsivity) diagnosis and place a check mark in the corresponding star.

If all diamonds in Attention Deficit and in Hyperactivity–Impulsivity are checked, consider ADHD Combined Type (Attention Deficit and Hyperactivity–Impulsivity) diagnosis and place a check mark in the corresponding star.

ADHD Predominantly Inattentive Type  **DIAGNOSIS**

ADHD Predominantly Hyperactive–Impulsive Type  **DIAGNOSIS**

ADHD Combined Type ■  **DIAGNOSIS**

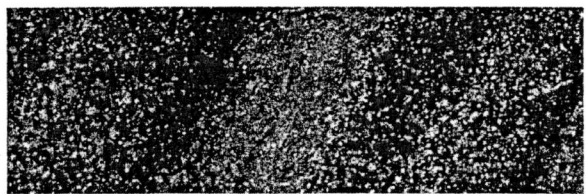

Screening Questions for Additional Childhood Disorders

This section contains screening questions for additional disorders that the interviewer might wish to pursue. The questions here are provided for the purpose of gathering basic information, not for establishing full diagnostic criteria. Further clinical inquiry will be necessary to confirm the presence of any of these disorders. If responses to questions in these categories indicate the need for further inquiry, the interviewer can circle the question mark at the end of each set of questions for each diagnostic category.

Substance Abuse

If the respondent is 11 years old or older or if you suspect the possibility of alcohol or other drug use in a younger child, ask Questions 1 and 2.

1. **Do you drink alcohol, like beer or wine?**   ☐ Yes ☐ No ☐ Other

   If "Yes," ask the child to elaborate. _____

   _____

   _____

2. **Do you smoke pot** (marijuana) **or use any other illegal drug?**   ☐ Yes ☐ No ☐ Other

   If "Yes," ask the child to elaborate. _____

   _____

   _____

 If the child responds "Yes" to Question 1 or 2 and the elaboration suggests a problem, ask Question 3. Otherwise, skip to Schizophrenia (p. 74).

3. **Have you ever been in trouble with your family, school, or police because of your use of** (name substance)?   ☐ Yes ☐ No ☐ Other

    If "Yes," ask, **What happened?** _____

_____

_____

If the child's responses suggest possible problems with substances, obtain further details, assess the current status, and take appropriate action.

If responses to Questions 1–3 warrant further clinical inquiry necessary to confirm Substance Abuse diagnosis, circle the question mark.

Substance Abuse

Schizophrenia

1a. **Have you ever heard voices when no one else was around?**   ☐ Yes ☐ No ☐ Other

1b. **Have you ever heard voices that no one else heard when other people were around?**   ☐ Yes ☐ No ☐ Other

    If the child responds "Yes" to either Question 1a or 1b, explain that this means actually hearing through the ears, as the child hears you, and not just a voice in the head, as one hears a thought. If this is the case, then count as a "Yes"; otherwise, do not.

2. **Have you ever seen things that were not really there?**   ☐ Yes ☐ No ☐ Other

3. **Do you get the feeling that people might do things behind your back to hurt you so that you need to be on the lookout?**   ☐ Yes ☐ No ☐ Other

4. **Do people tell you that they have trouble understanding you because you talk in a way that doesn't make sense?**   ☐ Yes ☐ No ☐ Other

If the child's responses suggest possible Schizophrenia, obtain further details, assess the current status, and take appropriate action.

If responses to Questions 1–4 warrant further clinical inquiry necessary to confirm Schizophrenia diagnosis, circle the question mark.

Schizophrenia

Selective Mutism

If the child has not responded verbally during the interview, it might be necessary to encourage the the child to use of the Feelings Thermometer or to nod yes or no to answer the following questions.

1. **Do you speak up at school when the teacher calls on you?** ☐ Yes ☐ No ☐ Other

2. **Do you talk to friends and other people who ask you questions?** ☐ Yes ☐ No ☐ Other

If "Yes" to Question 1 or 2, skip to Eating Disorders (p. 75).

If "No" to Questions 1 and 2, place a check mark in the diamond and continue.

CRITERION

3. **Do you talk with your family when you are at home?** ☐ Yes ☐ No ☐ Other

4. **Do you have any friends who speak for you? For instance, when you need something at school, do your friends ask for you?** ☐ Yes ☐ No ☐ Other

5. **Are things hard for you at school because you won't talk?** ☐ Yes ☐ No ☐ Other

6. **Are your parents upset because you won't speak to other people?** ☐ Yes ☐ No ☐ Other

7. **Have you ever spoken in school?** ☐ Yes ☐ No ☐ Other

   If "Yes," When did you stop? Did anything happen to upset you?

   _____

   _____

Diagnosis of Selective Mutism requires a failure to speak in selected situations, such as school, despite speaking in other situations; interference in functioning; and duration of at least 1 month. If the child's responses suggest Selective Mutism, obtain further details and take appropriate action.

If responses to Questions 1–7 warrant further clinical inquiry necessary to confirm Selective Mutism diagnosis, circle the question mark.

Selective Mutism ❓

Eating Disorders

1. **Do you think that your weight is what it should be for someone your age?** ☐ Yes ☐ No ☐ Other

2. **Do you wish that you could be thinner than you are now?** ☐ Yes ☐ No ☐ Other

3. **Do you worry a lot about your weight?** ☐ Yes ☐ No ☐ Other

4. **Do you find it hard to control your eating?** ☐ Yes ☐ No ☐ Other

5. **Do you have times when you go without eating** (fasting) **so that you can control your weight?** ☐ Yes ☐ No ☐ Other

6. **Do you ever find yourself eating a lot of food at one time?** ☐ Yes ☐ No ☐ Other

7. **People try all sorts of things to control or lose weight. They might go on diets, use medications, exercise for hours, or even try to vomit so that they don't gain any weight. Do you do anything like that to control your weight?** ☐ Yes ☐ No ☐ Other

   If "Yes" or "Other," **What kinds of things have you done in the past to control your weight?** _____

   _____

8. **What is your goal weight? Are you satisfied with your weight now?** ☐ Yes ☐ No ☐ Other

   _____

If the child's responses suggest a possible Eating Disorder, obtain further details and assess the current status.

If responses to Questions 1–8 warrant further clinical inquiry necessary to confirm Eating Disorder diagnosis, circle the question mark.

Eating Disorder

Somatoform Disorders

Hypochondriasis

1. **Are you always worrying that you might have a serious disease or illness** (e.g., cancer, AIDS, etc.)**?** ☐ Yes ☐ No ☐ Other

   If "Yes," **What types of diseases or illnesses do you think you might have?** _____

   _____

2. **Do you have any feelings** (symptoms) **or pains in your body that you think could be something serious?** ☐ Yes ☐ No ☐ Other

   If "Yes," **What feelings** (symptoms) **do you have?** _____

   _____

   How often do these feelings (symptoms) **happen to you?** _____

   _____

If "Yes" or unsure to either Question 1 or 2, continue. Otherwise, skip to Somatization Disorder (p. 77).

3. **Have you seen any doctors to find out what is wrong?**   ☐ Yes ☐ No ☐ Other

   If "Yes," **What did the doctor tell you?** _____

   _____

4. **If the doctor or your parent(s) tell you that everything is okay, that**   ☐ Yes ☐ No ☐ Other
   there is nothing wrong with you, do you believe them?

Somatization Disorder

1. **Do you have to go to the doctor a lot because of many different**   ☐ Yes ☐ No ☐ Other
   problems?

   If "Yes," **What kinds of problems have you had?** _____

   _____

 If "No," skip to Optional Interference Inquiry (p. 78).

Note. DSM–IV requires the following criteria for Somatization Disorder:

- Four pain symptoms (e.g., head, stomach, back, joints, extremities, chest, rectal, menstruation, or urination).
- Two gastrointestinal symptoms (e.g., nausea, diarrhea, bloating, vomiting, intolerance of several different foods).
- One sexual symptom (e.g., irregular menses, excessive menstrual bleeding).
- One pseudoneurological symptom (e.g., conversion symptoms, paralysis or localized weakness, difficulty swallowing or lump in throat, hearing loss, urinary retention, hallucinations, loss of touch or pain sensations, double vision, blindness, deafness, seizures).

2. **In what ways have these problems messed things up for you?**

   _____

   _____

If the child's responses suggest a possible Somatoform Disorder, obtain details and assess the current status.

If responses to Questions in the Hypchondriasis and Somatization sections warrant further clinical inquiry necessary to confirm Somatoform Disorder diagnosis, circle the question mark.

Somatoform Disorder

Optional Interference Inquiry

To identify specific areas of interference for any of the previously presented disorders, the interviewer may ask the following questions:

Does this problem mess things up for you at school? Think about whether it stops you from doing things at school and makes it hard for you to have fun at school. ☐ Yes ☐ No ☐ Other

Does this problem mess things up with friends? Think about whether it keeps you from making friends or doing things with friends. ☐ Yes ☐ No ☐ Other

Does this problem mess things up for you with your family? Think about whether it keeps you and your family from doing the things you would all like to do. ☐ Yes ☐ No ☐ Other

Does this problem mess things up for you, such as sleeping, eating, or concentrating on things like homework? Does it cause you to cry or to get upset easily? ☐ Yes ☐ No ☐ Other

For those questions to which the child responded "Yes" or "Other," inquire further to confirm that the child is referring to a clinically significant problem: **How does it interfere? What does it stop you from doing? What has it changed in your life?**

Child Initiated Topics (previously undiscussed)

1. **Of all the things that you talked about today, like** (give examples)**, which is the one problem that you would most like help with?** If the child responds "Nothing," inquire, **What do you think your parents want you to have help with?** _____

   _____

   _____

2. **Is there anything else that we should talk about? Anything that we haven't covered?**

   _____

   _____

   _____

   _____

   _____

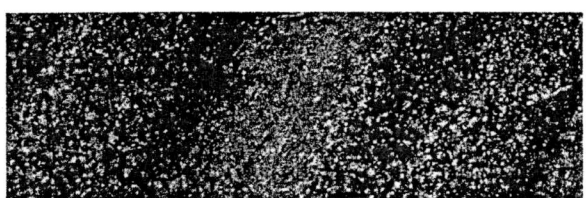

ADIS for DSM–IV:C
Child Interview
Schedule Summary

Name of Child _____

Name of Parent(s) _____

Interviewer _____

Interview Date _____

Interview Behavior

_____
_____
_____

Mental Status

_____
_____
_____

Psychosocial Stressors

The next series of questions are intended as a guide to assess the severity of psychosocial stressors. The interviewer should inquire about loss, parental divorce or separation, change in schools, and other specific stressors that might have an impact on the child's presenting complaint.

Think back over the past year. Have there been any problems or changes

a. **In your family?** _____
_____

b. **In your friendships?** _____

_____

c. **With school?** _____

_____

d. **With your health?** _____

_____

e. **With your parents' health or other family members' health?**

_____

_____

Narrative Summary

This summary should include presenting complaint, history, diagnostic impression, and information obtained from the previous questions. _____

_____

_____

_____

_____

_____

_____

_____

_____

_____

Summary of Current *DSM-IV* Diagnoses and Clinician Severity Rating

The clinician's severity rating (CSR) is based on the following 9-point scale (0–8) and is guided by the child's interference ratings, total number of symptoms endorsed, and clinician's impression for each diagnostic category.

	Principle Diagnosis	Clinician's Severity Rating	Additional Diagnoses	Clinician's Severity Rating
Axis I	_____	_____	_____	_____
	_____	_____	_____	_____
	_____	_____	_____	_____
Axis II	_____	_____	_____	_____
Axis III	_____	_____	_____	_____
Axis IV	_____	_____	_____	_____
Axis V	Present _____		Last Year _____	

ABSENT	MILD	MODERATE	SEVERE	VERY SEVERE
0	1 ▬ 2 ▬ 3	4 ▬ 5	6 ▬ 7	8
None	Slightly Disturbing/ Not Really Disabling	Definitely Disturbing/ Disabling	Markedly Disturbing/ Disabling	Very Severely Disturbing/ Disabling

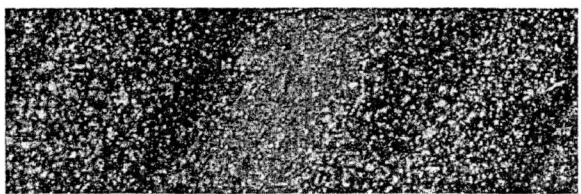

Clinician's Composite Summary Based on ADIS for DSM–IV:C Child Interview Schedule and Parent Interview Schedule

Name of Child_____

Name of Parent(s)_____

Interviewer_____

Interview Date_____

Current *DSM–IV* Diagnoses and Clinician Severity Rating

The clinician's severity rating (CSR) is based on the following 9-point scale (0–8) and is guided by the parent's interference ratings, total number of symptoms endorsed, and clinician's impression for each diagnostic category.

	Principle Diagnosis	Clinician's Severity Rating	Additional Diagnoses	Clinician's Severity Rating
Axis I	_____	_____	_____	_____
	_____	_____	_____	_____
Axis II	_____	_____	_____	_____
Axis III	_____	_____	_____	_____
Axis IV	_____	_____	_____	_____
Acute	_____			
Enduring	_____			
Stressors	_____			

	Principle Diagnosis	Clinician's Severity Rating	Additional Diagnoses	Clinician's Severity Rating
Axis V	_____	_____	_____	_____
Present	_____			
Last Year	_____			

ABSENT	MILD	MODERATE	SEVERE	VERY SEVERE

0 ▨▨▨ 1 ▨▨▨ 2 ▬▬▬ 3 ▬▬▬ 4 ▬▬▬ 5 ▬▬▬ 6 ▬▬▬ 7 ▬▬▬ 8

None	Slightly Disturbing/ Not Really Disabling	Definitely Disturbing/ Disabling	Markedly Disturbing/ Disabling	Very Severely Disturbing/ Disabling

Calendar—Side 1

Month 1

Week	Monday	Tuesday	Wednesday	Thursday	Friday	Saturday	Sunday
Week 1							
Week 2							
Week 3							
Week 4							

Month 2

Week	Monday	Tuesday	Wednesday	Thursday	Friday	Saturday	Sunday
Week 1							
Week 2							
Week 3							
Week 4							

Month 3

Week	Monday	Tuesday	Wednesday	Thursday	Friday	Saturday	Sunday
Week 1							
Week 2							
Week 3							
Week 4							

Calendar—Side 2

January
S	M	T	W	T	F	S
---	---	---	---	---	---	---

February
S	M	T	W	T	F	S
---	---	---	---	---	---	---

March
S	M	T	W	T	F	S
---	---	---	---	---	---	---

April
S	M	T	W	T	F	S
---	---	---	---	---	---	---

May
S	M	T	W	T	F	S
---	---	---	---	---	---	---

June
S	M	T	W	T	F	S
---	---	---	---	---	---	---

July
S	M	T	W	T	F	S
---	---	---	---	---	---	---

August
S	M	T	W	T	F	S
---	---	---	---	---	---	---

September
S	M	T	W	T	F	S
---	---	---	---	---	---	---

October
S	M	T	W	T	F	S
---	---	---	---	---	---	---

November
S	M	T	W	T	F	S
---	---	---	---	---	---	---

December
S	M	T	W	T	F	S
---	---	---	---	---	---	---